§

Listen to Your Elders

Writing from Litquake Elder Project 2023

Edited by

Kevin Dublin Tam Putnam

San Francisco

ISBN: 978-1-93-584719-9

Library of Congress Cataloging-in-Publication Data on file
Library of Congress Control Number: 2024930077

Litquake, ATTN: Elder Project Permissions, 268 Bush St #4226, San Francisco, CA 94104 or Etched Press, ATTN: Permissions, permissions@etchedpress.com.

Elder Project, is a year-round project of the Litquake Foundation, a 501(c)3 nonprofit registered in the state of California and gratefully acknowledges support from: California Arts Council, Joseph & Vera Long Foundation, and Yerba Buena Center for the Arts. Learn more at **www.litquake.org/elderproject.html.**

The Living Room SF produces engaging community experiences, publications, and fosters partnerships to develop economic opportunities for Bay Area writers with unstable incomes and a primary focus on BIPOC writers to cultivate literary community. Learn more at **www.thelivingroomsf.org.**

Book Design by Kevin Dublin
Cover Photo: "Embarcadero Sunrise" by Kevin Dublin

Printed in the United States of America
First Edition 2023

§

for Jessie Scrimager Galloway

founder & shining light

Table of Contents

Dr. George Davis Senior Center 1

Don Collier **2**

1962 Road Trip 3

Franklin Curry **11**

When I'm Home 13
Origins 14

Samuel Chilton **16**

It was Only a Dream 17
When I'm Home 18

Matthew Greer **19**

When I'm Home 20
Where Did the Time Go? 21

Wanda Greer **25**

Waiting 26
The Pressure of Loss 27

Frank Residences at the SFCJL 29

Fredi Aks **30**

A Love Match? 31
Blueberry Surprise! 33
At 84 35

Esther Mugar **37**

Necessity Is the Mother of Invention 38
A Fairy Tale for the Modern Woman 42
Day Camp 46

Corrine Sacks **48**

New York Beach 49

Stuart Span **51**

A Freeway Through the Street 52
In the Navy 53
Old Lady Nature 54
A Great Man 55
Richmond, Virginia, 1942 56

Michael Thaler **57**

Birthplace 58
My German Lessons 60

Janet Underwood **64**

Middle Name 65
Koko and Me 66

Community Living Campaign: Cayuga Connectors *69*

Elina Adams **70**

Rant 71

Jane Alexander **72**

The Fall 73

Beth Arnaoot **75**

Ode to Hopscotch 76

Doris Beers **78**

Just Three Knocks 79
The Wrong Journey 81
After Surgery 82
Sunday after Midnight 84

Naomi Cooper **87**
Ode to the Upstairs Neighbor Dog 88
Love Song Riding 90
Surrender 92
Grace D'Anca **93**
I Wanted to Know How It Would End 94
Queen Casey 95
Something Sometimes 96
If We Don't Speak 98
Helen Dannenberg **100**
Hello New Poetry 101
A Plan 103
Eureka: I Found It 104
Paco Lorenzo Melgar **106**
Occasion 107
"Best of" New Year's List 108
Joe Ochab **109**
Dancing with the "You" and the "I" … 110
Lee Ellen Shoemaker **114**
Bunker Hill Air Force Base, Summer 1957 115
Summer Games 116
Greg Taylor (aka Horehound Stillpoint) **120**
I Was Told by Forces I Do Not Understand … 121
Lucky Son of a Bundle of Nerves 125
If I Die Tonight, at Least … This 128
Mary Gayle Thomas **130**
The Force 131

The Crazy Part 134
Return 137

Roger Underhill 139

Rock, Stones, and Gems of Our Lives 140
Is That You, Mr. Martin? 142

Downtown Oakland Senior Center 147

Kittye Winn 148

Running Away 149
Bless the Mess 150
To Become a Poet 152
Hell's Cool Midst 154

Tanna Bellia 156

She Plays All Day 157
Where Do I Dwell if not in Possibility? 159
I Am 161
She Was 162

Zakiyyah G.E. Capehart 163

A Tragic Accident 164

Mark F. DeWitt 166

What Is a Cross? 167

D. Fromm 169

Cars Poetica 170
Engraved 171

Julie R. Hawthorne 174

Notes from Memorial Day 2023 175

Irene Kane **177**
Tired Peonies (Memory and Gratitude) 178
Journeys 181
Irene Sardanis **184**
Kathy, the Bead Lady 185
Trickster 188
Greek Easter 190
The Past 193
Paula J. Shadle **194**
The Street Booth 195
Coming to America 199
Hospice 203
Susan Steinhauer **207**
The Gift 208
Barbara Tooma **211**
The Portrait 212
In the Hospital 213
Former Self, Present Self 214

Community Living Campaign: Bethel Church *217*

Christine Arenas **218**
Seasons of the City 219
Victoria Hamilton **220**
Lady Cat 221
About the Anthology **223**

§

Dr. George Davis Senior Center

Don Collier

Don Collier is a retired railroad worker.

1962 Road Trip

"I got the feeling there's a roadblock down this road. I'm going take the back roads," declared my Uncle Roy. The local sheriff's roadblock was just as much a custom in these parts as driving around with open cans of beer and firearms. It was just a simple matter of inconvenience or not.

I saw nothing up ahead, but at that time my head was only slightly higher than the dashboard. I heard my two sisters stirring in the back seat. But what they saw, what they thought, what they were stirring about was no concern of mine. They were just there, two sisters in the back seat. What I wanted was the hamburgers Uncle Roy had promised to treat us to. In my head I rehearsed a plea for a vanilla malt and, just maybe, french fries. These were my favorite three foods. They were not so easily come by; the chain of Golden Arches was still far from reaching this part of the country. I had tasted one of those over-one-million-sold and was unimpressed. Old-fashion drive-up roadside burger stand was the very best, right-off-the-grill burger patties and buns, just the right amount of lettuce, tomato, and onion. A touch of mayonnaise on the bun, not the patty—a piece of lettuce should be between the two—and ketchup to smother the fries.

So, with these great concerns, I asked "Why?"

"Because this is something they just do to mess with people. And I don't want to be bothered with them. I know all these back roads. We'll just go 'round them."

"OK," I said. I knew that white police (Black police being a rarity) were mean people not to be trusted; Black police I soon learned were no different. I figured it was best to avoid them, especially the Black cop out to prove himself. Avoiding was different from running. My mom had told me never to run from the police because they would shoot a Black boy. It didn't matter what you did or didn't do.

"Don't run!" she said. "Tell 'em you need your mother and keep your mouth shut after that. Don't give 'em any lip and make 'em mad." Uncle Roy was not running; he was avoiding. That was OK.

Uncle Roy was a sophisticated man of the world. He knew when to avoid and when to not run. He was the only Black man that we knew in the U.S. Air Force. And top of all that he did paperwork, not sweat work. He traveled the world from Germany to Merced, California. As I grew older, grew embarrassed about his strong patriotism, he would say, "The white Jim Crow segregationists were un-American and we Negroes were the only true patriots defending democracy."

Whenever he came to visit, he had a new car, such as the Impala with fins. The new car was always accompanied with a new woman friend—sometimes introduced as his wife, meaning we had to call her Aunt.

He smoked a pipe with fragrant tobacco. He cared for his pipes with a most interesting assortment of tools to "keep the pipe fresh." The pocketknife-size stainless steel tool was a three-in-one: a tamper to pack tobacco in the bowl, a small pick and knife to remove encrusted ash. There was an old silver lighter shaped like a large tube of lipstick; pulled apart, the connected halves opened a fire chamber in the center. Most intriguing were the slender white bristle-wire stems that traveled up the shank; when withdrawn the white was gradations of brownest reaching toward a gooey black tar tip. He was the only man who did such a thing—cigarette smoking had little refinement in comparison with Uncle Roy's pipe.

He wore dress pants, dress shirts, polished shoes with silk socks, and a wisp of Old Spice cologne. All this dressed a frame of muscle, dark brown skin, clean shiny nails, and a fresh haircut. How did he keep his clothes so clean and pressed at all times? Uncle Roy's women came and went with regularity. I had an older sister who did this work until wash-and-wear clothes came along. After this I always wore my clothes a little wrinkled. Nobody but me seemed to notice.

All other family adults—uncles, aunts, cousins, grandparents, and my parents too—showed their country roots. If they lived in a city they had a look, a sign of sorts, that said, "I Just Got Here from the Country." If they lived in the northeast, north, or like us, California, this sign would have a kicker, "I'm from the South." Their lives were more accustomed to outhouses, wood-burning stoves, pulling up well water. Indoor plumbing and gas heat were new in their lives. But Uncle Roy seemed he had lived all his life knowing nothing of outhouse stink, heating water on the stove for the tin bathtub, snakes and mice everywhere. He seemed to be quite different, and he was.

He had my full trust as far as the roadblock went. Uncle Roy was not the type to cross the law. He was a military man; extremely patriotic. As the car turned off the blacktop main road onto the back road, kicking up gravel and dust, I had my misgivings. There would be no burger stands down this way, that much I knew. If anything appeared it would be a juke joint with cold drinks and barbecue. I preferred a hamburger with the works to such fare any day. But I did not complain. Uncle Roy always kept his promise—especially with treats for us kids. I kept a diligent eye out for any prospect.

We rode up and down the gentle rolling hills of middle Tennessee, around curves thick with trees. The road appeared to end at these curves only to present itself again after the turn. The sound of rubber meeting gravel rock was soothing. The woods were impenetrable with green and shadow overlapping. Then I spiedspy an open space just ahead. Promise. Sniffed the air for the inviting aroma of burger. What came instead was another inviting wonderful smell, tobacco leaves drying. The tobacco barn stood off to the right in the clearing; front and back fully open, sides half open. To smell air-cured tobacco fragrant and sweet, to see the rich brown broad leaf was a delight. However, it was no substitute for burgers. We drove on and on. Then finally gravel gave way to blacktop, a main road, a sure sign of a promise fulfilled. Confident that the roadblock was behind us we drove on.

More woods thick with green and shadow. An expanse of lawn this time with a single story red brick house. The red brick meant that the family were doing well. The same size wooden house painted white was a notch down. The family must be white as this rural area surely was. Black homes were smaller, and unpainted wood. The more prosperous Black family home was a little bigger, still wood, but painted white. Red brick for Blacks was middle class; they were counted in ones and twos. We drove on under the green and shadow of woods. Black asphalt stretching forward for us to catch up to; only stretched out more, even curving this way and that.

"There's one!" I spotted a roadside stand, semicircular, painted red, several service windows facing a small hardened dirt parking lot. Adjacent to it was a gas station which by its red paint seemed to be part of the business.

"We can't stop here," Uncle Roy said.

"Why?"

"Because colored folks are not allowed in this town."

But my mind and body were on the little red burger stand. For emphasis Uncle Roy added, "We can't even stop here for gas."

He continued to drive on as I looked at the last glimpse of the stand.

"What if we run out of gas?" I asked.

"We're not going to run out of gas."

I was silent. Uncle Roy had the last word. I pondered for years after on this question—what if we ran out of gas in a town that did not allow colored folks? I had no sense of violence; all I knew was schoolyard fights of children.

I imagine walking with Uncle Roy, gas can in hand to the pump. A grizzled white man comes out of the gas station store, says, "I ain't gonna sell y'all gas, colored ain't allowed in this town." I smell the aroma of cooking burger patties, but there is no hope now. The car is slowly moving, pushed by Uncle Roy, toward a sign marking the town boundary. I'm in the driver's seat steering it straight; pretending to drive was my next favorite thing to hamburgers.

Franklin Curry

Born August 4th, 1934 in Ocala, Florida, Franklin D. Roosevelt Curry has lived in San Francisco since he hitchhiked across the country, earning a living since June 1959. He has great love for God, his wife, and people.

Smooth

To me, smooth is when you can learn something when you don't know how to read and write. It takes time.

I came here in June 1959. The more I get around to meet people, talk to people. I know I'm learning something. I ain't been here 88 years for nothing.

I've got to know something. When you learn, no one can take it from you. You gotta keep it in your head. That's how I learned about people around in the Bay Area.

It was hard. It was really hard to do, but I learned how to take care of myself. And I've been here for almost 88 years, you know, I know a little bit about loving people.

I speak to people because, like my mama said, "when you keep your mouth closed, you won't learn nothing." So I talk to people and learn from them, and I've been doing alright.

My name is Franklin. D. Roosevelt Curry. And that's my story.

When I'm Home

for Sally Curry

When I'm home, I can hear my TV on a station, my wife's sickness, her lungs in four stages and the sound of "I lost this" and "I lost that," my medicine and her mind not together.

When I'm home, I can smell everything normal without upsetting her or the rush back to the hospital and 7 years of marriage.

When I'm home, I help her clean. She's been smoking since 1959 on Fillmore and Eddy.

When I'm home, I feel like I'm a man, and I feel like she'll never cheat on me. I'll never cheat on her.

And when I'm home I can taste perfect, and I can share my perfect taste or my voice.

When I'm home I like to talk. I like to talk. I like to meet people.

In this world, you've got to know people. You can't live in this world by yourself.

Origins

Born August 4th, 1934 in Ocala, Florida

Life was simple back when I was a child.
I was the youngest of eleven children:
Five boys and six girls,
And sometimes that was good,
  and sometimes it was bad.

We were all taught right from wrong.
Didn't have time to be well educated, though,
But had a mother wit more sense than those who did.
I ain't saying anything wrong with having an education.
Just seems it don't necessarily make you a better person.
It's good for getting better jobs, though.

All my sisters and brothers left Ocala,
Left me with my ailing mother.
I worked to take care of her since I was a teen,
Wanted to learn how to read,
but never got the chance.
Mother died…
I injured my back.
Doctors removed four discs and

replaced them with plastic discs.
Right shoulder and arm
still numb and tinglin' down my leg,
But I thank the Lord.
He continues to make a way.

I sold vegetables from my garden just
A few hundred feet from the highway.
I'd display 'em where the people could see.
They'd pull over, park the car
And come over to buy some.
I'd make a little money like that,
but I got to thinking that
I'm barely surviving.
I can't stay in Ocala.
I got to make a better way,
And I did.
I came to California.

Samuel Chilton

Samuel lives and writes in San Francisco.

It was Only a Dream

As I began to run my hand over the surface I noticed how smooth it was but it seemed as if everyone around me was looking as if I was flirting with them. As the rain fell, it created a puddle I could hear as the rain splashed into it. Standing under a streetlight, I cast a shadow. I was always amazed at how much bigger it was than I. Sitting there, I was trying to think of a way I could make some sweet scratch. Nothing came to mind. Then I heard a loud crinkle. It was at that moment I realized I was dreaming.

When I'm Home

When I'm home, I can hear the train as it
passes, and people as they talk and laugh.

When I'm home, I can smell flowers in the
garden or fresh air and car exhaust.

When I'm home, I see blue sky and flowers
from the back patio, but never fights and
never car crashes.

When I'm home, I feel like I'm safe; I feel good
about life.

Matthew Greer

Matthew Greer, born and raised in the historic Fillmore District of San Francisco, is an active participant and leader in the Elder Project. He brings stories of family, growth, hustle, sobriety and growing older. He also read his poems at RAWdance's 2022 event "Step/Song/Story."

When I'm Home

When I'm home, I can hear my TV on and can
also hear my wife asking me to do something
and the days all go better with understanding
in the home.

When I'm home, I can smell food on the stove,
sweet soft perfume or flowers in the wind
and just the smell of good living.

When I'm home, I see comfort and feel
comfortable but never uncomfortable and
never have the sorry feeling of sadness.

When I'm home, I feel like a king on the
throne, just alright, and I feel like I made this
home the way it is.

And when I'm home, I can taste realness, love
in my house, and I can share feelings or
whatever I have. When I'm home.

Where Did the Time Go?

I remember running to the store with my big brother
To get a box of cereal, and on the way,
There'd be that cherry tree.
Any time we had to go to the store and
  The cherries were ready,
    We'd eat from that tree until we got full
      But where did the time go?

It has been said time waits for nobody.
So true!
Another saying is,
Enjoy every day because before you know it
  You'll be older and wiser and
    Stop making stupid mistakes
      That get you in jail or in hell.

It's all about the people you meet
Going from place to place.
You remember their names from an early age
Starting school, going to classes,
Learning different things,
Getting us prepared for our lives

and the surprises ahead of us.
  Sports played a big role in our scheduled days
    But where did the time go?

Then girls came into our lives.
We see a different change in ourselves.
  We'd never be the same ever again.
With this, driving, buying a car, clothes and jewelry,
    along with moving out, made our lives whiz by…
Time seemed to fly by faster and faster,
Learning as we grew older time never stops
We just enjoyed ourselves.
Respected those who respected us

Then we began fatherhood and motherhood,
Having children at an early age.
Then came the real learning,
    Responsibility
Thinking not only of ourselves,
    But other mouths to feed.
I'm 16 going on 17 years-old.

I knew a few things
Was a hustler since I could remember

So it was time to get busy and work a little harder
And stay out of juvie or jail

Did what I was good at
Did my best to keep it crackin'
Did whatever it took to put food on the table
And keep money in my pockets.

Between hustling and working,
I always had some kind of habit
To keep me going on the side
Coke, weed, alcohol
I kept it close at all times…
Then it got real old!

Found myself in AA meetings,
Jail, and the hospitals where
Things began to make good sense to me
Sobriety now a big part of my life.
I found a way to get my life back
Keep my head up…

Love life on life's terms!

Time waits for nobody and nothing,
So we keep ourselves in good shape.
Take care of our responsibilities,
As we keep on growing
  Older and older and older…
    Where did the time go?

Wanda Greer

Originally from eastern North Carolina, Wanda 'Cricket' Greer, is a poet, proud mother and grandmother who writes about family and the world.

Waiting

The stars were a trickle above the shining sky. I had to chalk my mind around how beautiful they were. I was thinking they were so bright I might have to find some shade to cover myself, and I didn't want to rip my clothes in the dark. I was waiting, so I could get a little sunsplash of daylight.

The Pressure of Loss

The pressure of loss—
losing loved ones,
the memories of my father.
I couldn't attend his funeral,
so my youngest sister sends
a cell phone picture of his casket.
My father seemed to be standing by it,
an angel from heaven,
but it's not him … it's my brother.
The DNA deep in our family tree.
Brother holds strong our father's genes.

The pressures of loss:
losing loved ones,
the memories
of my brother-in-law,
my best friend,
my brother from another mother—
someone I could trust with my life.
I can still see him when I watch
Subway or Starbuck commercials.
The laughs we had on his porch outside or

seeing hummingbirds or an ageless man
 or paintings of African settings.

The pressures of loss…
losing loved ones,
my son
named after both his grandfathers.
I can still feel him
 when I see cozy blankets
  or smell the scent of baby powder.
Too much to bear here in one year.
The loss of loved ones,
the memories

I'm still here to tell,
still have to tell—
God is great!

§

Frank Residences at the San Francisco Campus for Jewish Living

Fredi Aks

Fredi Aks' 84 years consist of 20 years on the East Coast, 20 years in the Midwest, 20 years in Southern California, and another 20 in the San Francisco Bay Area, with some foreign travel sprinkled in for good measure. She's had the opportunity to experience, learn, and enjoy a lot.

A Love Match?

A street in the poor part of Baltimore on a hot summer day. A handsome young man stands outside a tobacco shop, leaning against the store window. Several of his friends are nearby and engaged in conversation, but he is not interested. He looks, in profile, like Rudolph Valentino, and he knows it, adjusting his slouch to increase the effect as he puffs on his cigarette.

Close, a slightly chubby young girl stands with another group, but her gaze frequently turns toward the cigarette store. She wears a light-colored cotton dress that moves in the summer breeze, and wisps from a curly mop of hair stick to her forehead and neck. She is carrying a bag of large, sweet green grapes and she plucks one and holds it between her teeth before she chews.

She takes three steps toward the young man, who is watching her now. "Would you like a grape?" she says, wondering if she looks like Theda Bara, as she straightens her dress with her hand. He smiles, flicks the cigarette like Valentino, and accepts the grape.

This is how my parents met. Each was from a family with 10 children, my father the eldest in his, my mother the youngest in hers. Their families had arrived in Baltimore at the turn of the century, and they both considered themselves Americans. I don't know how their relationship continued, or when they got married. I remember hearing about a trip to Ellicott City, Maryland, a town famous for instant weddings, but I can't connect it to the two of them.

There must have been a period when they displayed affection for each other, but by the time I was old enough to notice, their only form of discourse was argument. If divorce had been as available and acceptable then as it is now, I am sure I would not be here to write about their meeting.

Blueberry Surprise!

In the days before car navigation systems, our children got used to hearing my husband say, "Day trip! Grab your stuff! We're heading out of Illinois." The four of us would pile into the Jeep Wagoneer, and whoever was elected navigator would find the map book and track our journey.

One year, friends had told us that Indiana was famous for its blueberry crop, and since it was blueberry picking season, I guessed our destination would be wherever those blueberries were. It was warm and sunny and the highway was uncrowded. Once we crossed the state line into Indiana, signs on side roads led us: "Pick blueberries here. Buy 'em by the bucket. Turn right in 200 feet." When we stopped, the children pulled us to the nearest stand, stacked with cardboard containers. We each took a stack and headed out to the bushes, where other families were already filling their own baskets. We began with the largest berries, on bushes near the back of the field (one berry for the mouth, one for the basket). After about 30 minutes, we slowed down a bit, and I heard music coming over loudspeakers.

I glanced to the end of the field, where a chain-link fence stretched around the perimeter. Beyond was a large swimming pool surrounded by beach umbrellas and tables. Twenty or thirty people lounged at the tables, and others were dancing to the music. It took me several minutes to realize that while they all wore hats and sandals, none of them had on a stitch of clothing. Our children were still happily plucking blueberries when I tapped my husband's shoulder and motioned for him to look past the fence.

He smiled broadly, then said, "OK kids, time to go. Let's get those baskets into the car and head home to bake some pies." And just like that, we drove back. As the kids carried the blueberry baskets into the house, my husband said softly to me, "Indiana is also famous for its nudist colonies. Didn't know they'd put one in blueberry country. Just think of it as an extra delight."

At 84

My daughter recently said to me, "Your children are grown, your husband and his illnesses are behind you, and now you can make choices you wouldn't have made earlier in your life. What do you want to be when you grow up?" I'm trying to figure out the answer to that question.

I am 84 years old, but it's difficult to adjust to that. In the last year, I have had to respond to the loss of my husband of 61 years. I've kept myself occupied with meaningful work, and have remained physically active in spite of aches and pains. I find it easy to forget that I can't walk briskly or bend down to retrieve something that has fallen to the floor. The daily reminders, from twinges to grimaces, help me remember.

I am happy that my mental abilities, though slipping ever so slightly, are still sound. It drives me crazy when I misplace something, but it happens less frequently now that I have fewer things to keep track of. I have begun to depend on equipment I never thought I'd need—a walker, an iPhone to help me remember appointments, a chair in the shower. I have given up driving because I can't trust my reflexes, and miss taking long rides in open country. I've had to curb my once hearty appetite, not for beauty but for health's sake. I've also become accustomed to having white hair, and keep it cut short to require less styling. I no longer recognize the face I see in the mirror.

Aging has given me the luxury of time to review what has been really important in my life. For the most part, I find I would change very little of my past.

My fondest memories take me back to when my children were small and family life was active and noisy and happy, when I felt necessary and capable and emotionally in control. I love those memories. I'm happy to still be here, aches and all—the alternative only a glimmer on the horizon. I'm determined to enjoy the time I have left with those I cherish and who care for me.

Esther Mugar

Born and bred in the Bronx, New York, Esther Mugar had a childhood shaped by the standards of the '50s and a consciousness by the cultural upheaval of the '60s. Travel has always brought her joy and inspiration. She loved to wander and see what the day would bring. When a massive stroke incapacitated her, that life ended. Now she paints and writes. It's a new existence, but she's trying to make it work.

Necessity Is the Mother of Invention

It was early evening when the steamer docked in Yokohama. For some time I had been watching the glow of the city lights grow brighter on the horizon as the voyage from Siberia came to an end. This city was huge, overwhelming after the restful train ride spanning several days and four time zones from Moscow, across the vast taiga forest and along the shore of Lake Baikal before arriving in Nahodka (at that time the only eastern port of the U.S.S.R. open to foreigners), followed by the sea crossing to Yokohama.

I was nervous. Japan was bustling and expensive, exciting yet intimidating. I was a weary backpacker with limited funds that shrank by the day as the yen climbed against the dollar, with three weeks to go before my flight home to San Francisco. I had sublet my apartment to a Japanese student studying English. Her friend Jonny, who had recently returned to Yokohama, agreed to meet me at the dock. How would I find him in this crowd? Would he even come? As my eyes scanned the throng, I heard my name shouted out and there he was, waving frantically in his Mickey Mouse shirt. My nervousness turned to joy as I disembarked. Jonny, as excited as I was, gave me a crash course in this foreign culture, showing me how to walk through the crowds, how to find small, unmarked eateries with good cheap food, how to negotiate transit, and how to find street addresses (the building numbers went around each block). By the following day I felt confident enough to head for Tokyo, the address of a student hostel in hand.

The hostel was clean but basic, with dorm rooms for each gender and a traditional bathroom for each. The only other females in residence were a group of teenage students. One was preoccupied with pressing her pleated skirt under her mattress, and two others with applying makeup, but I was by far the biggest attraction. It's doubtful that they had seen naturally curly hair gone wild before and they were clearly impressed. There was much giggling and pointing until I invited them to comb it and watch it spiral back on itself. That broke the ice, but not enough for me to share a traditional bath with them. I waited until they were asleep to get clean. The bathroom had water spigots spaced along the walls about a foot above the cement floor with a bucket and a tiny stool by each. The idea was to soap up, then fill your bucket from the spigot to rinse off. Only when clean could you get in the communal pool. The soak was glorious and I slept like a baby that night, but the next day I knew that I would have to wash my hair. But how?

After breakfast I had a walk around the neighborhood. When I returned, the gardener was watering carefully manicured shrubs around the entrance. His hose was cracked and leaking. As I watched, he cut the hose at the crack and left about two feet to dispose of later. In my well-practiced pantomime I asked if I could have the remnant. He handed it to me with that "crazy American" look I had seen many times before. I ran my treasure inside. The girls were gone. The bathroom was all mine. And, wouldn't you know, the end of that hose fit the spigot perfectly and I was able to shampoo all the grime of the past week out of my naturally curly hair. I carried that hose with me all through the country. Many adventures followed but I always had clean hair.

Necessity is the mother of invention.

A Fairy Tale for the Modern Woman

Once upon a time there was a beautiful young girl with golden hair, deep blue eyes, and a gentle spirit, who charmed everyone she met. Her friends idolized her. She rewarded them with a sprinkle of her homemade pixie dust guaranteed to make kale (in vogue at the moment) taste like chocolate. Her teachers fawned over her. Upon completing her education, she became spokesperson for the Pure Delight Ice Cream Company, known for its fat-free, sugar-free, all-natural, zero-calorie exquisitely flavored treats. Her photo graced every container. When she outgrew that image, she made a name for herself at the Telekinesis Institute designing luxury time-travel transporters. But this was just a prelude to her true life's work, the rehabilitation of wayward trolls.

Trolls are known for their unnerving charm. Although not fair of face and form, their self-confidence and gift of gab make them irresistible to women lacking a certain sophistication in matters of the heart. Their rehabilitation involves therapy to find the spark of compassion lurking deep within the psyche of all creatures and to cultivate it until a conscience begins to develop. This requires both focus and great patience on the part of the therapist. Our heroine's kindness and unfaltering dedication made her an icon in the field.

Of course suitors pursued her. One had a title and a castle with a moat—too patrician. Another ran an exclusive eco-lodge in the rainforest—too remote. One dressed impeccably and spoke six languages—too haughty. One wore black leather and rode a Harley. He just smelled bad. No one could capture our heroine's heart, but her fame and status more than sustained her. The world was hers.

Until... One day a raven-haired beauty arrived on the scene. She had piercing green eyes, porcelain skin, and the grace of a ballerina. Tentatively auditioning as an actress, she soon took Hollywood by storm, appearing on the cover of every major magazine. She developed a huge following, which supported her foray into the world of fashion and beauty products.

Soon her image was everywhere. As the world's attention shifted, our heroine lost her edge. Try as she might, she couldn't regain her place in the spotlight.

Until... Our heroine frequently visited a small rocky beach to clear her head and reflect on her change of fortune. One day she found a luminous stone glowing brightly at her feet. She picked it up and felt heat coming from within. As she dropped it in surprise, she heard a voice saying, "You have awakened me, sweet girl. How can I help you?" She excitedly imagined the possibilities. Was this a genie who could grant her heart's desire, heap vengeance upon her nemesis, and restore her own former glory? But our heroine was not naive. There must be a catch, she thought. Will I be sacrificing my soul, my youth, my self-respect? What should I do? She pondered and pondered until darkness fell and the stone turned opaque, blending in with all the other stones on the beach.

Here's where the epilogue and the moral of this tale should appear. But that, dear reader, is up to you. Will our heroine continue on her life's path to make the world a better place? Or will she return home dejected, her resolve weakened, and begin a tragic downward spiral? And what will befall her nemesis? Does she marry a troll who depletes her fortune and effectively ends her brilliant career, or does she achieve even greater fame, marry well, produce clever, gorgeous children, and live a happy, fulfilled life for many decades to come? The choice is yours.

Day Camp

What new horror was this? I'd been perfectly content to spend my long summer days building Lego castles with Mary Ann from next door, or engrossed in a good book (Nancy Drew my series of choice), but my parents, caring and well-meaning, thought that a supervised outdoor experience would contribute to my health and well-being.

The volunteer who escorted us to the camp was a neighborhood high schooler. We rode two subway trains, transferring mid-trip, to get to Fort Washington Park, at the foot of the George Washington Bridge. Wooded trails led down to the Hudson River, but poison ivy cautioned us to stay with the group. There were games and songs and a boxed lunch. I hated it. Each evening I asked my parents not to send me back.

"Just finish out the week," they answered. "You might change your mind." I didn't.

One day, while the others were engrossed in some inane activity, I just left. I confidently walked the several blocks to the subway station, dropped my token into the slot, pushed through the turnstile, and followed the route so familiar to me by now—downtown A train to 145th Street, change to the uptown D train, and then straight home. I felt very grown up and in control, until I reached my front door, where I found my distraught parents—why were they so upset?—and the parents of the teenaged volunteer. Why were they here? Then I saw the policeman. My resolve crumbled and my knees started to shake. Was I in trouble? When had they noticed that I had left? And why did they doubt that I could find my way home? I realized they all thought I had been kidnapped or worse and were genuinely worried, so worried that they forgot to punish me.

I never went back to camp.

Corrine Sacks

A third-generation New Yorker, Corrine Sacks was born in Brooklyn, and later lived on the Upper West Side of Manhattan for 47 years. Twenty years ago, she moved to San Francisco to be close to her children.

New York Beach

I was among the lucky ones—we lived near the ocean, at the end of Coney Island in Brooklyn. It was lovely year round—even in fall, when hurricanes drove the water up the street in great waves. But in summer, in those years without air conditioning, living one block from the water was a privilege. As a teenager, it was obligatory to spend as much time as possible on the beach with your friends, gossiping, criticizing, and generally being obnoxious, as teenagers will.

Being a member of the herd required me to be there—and I dutifully put on my bathing suit, got my blanket, and out I went. I always carried a small bottle of oil mixed with iodine. You see, I have skin that turns red and blisters in the sun. There was no sunscreen then, and I used this concoction in an attempt to coat the skin so it wouldn't burn. I loved the water and when I wasn't talking to my friends or flirting with the gangly, big-footed, awkward boys who were trying to get our attention, I would spend all the time in the water. I swam like a fish, loved riding the waves, and floating back from wherever those waves took me.

But I paid a price for this pleasure with shoulders coated with salt, blisters, and red, peeling skin. One year I had a Saturday night date with a good-looking guy who was willing to travel to my house (in those days the boy came and picked you up, and returned you to your parents later that night). This guy would have to take a subway train and two buses to get to my house. No mean feat, this showed sincere interest. I left the beach early to prepare for my big date.

After showering, I made a terrible discovery—my shoulders were so sore, red, and blistered that I couldn't stand having the slightest pressure on them—no bra, no cloth, nothing. Mom and I picked out a sundress that would work with a strapless bra, but the pain was so bad that Mom had to cover my shoulders with vinegar to soothe them.

So there I was—dressed up, hair and makeup perfect, and smelling like a pickle.

Stuart Span

Stuart Span grew up in Richmond, Virginia. When he turned 18, he signed up on the first day of the draft for the Korean War. He spent three years in the Navy in a security position. Afterwards, he studied horticulture at the University of Maryland before moving to Southern California where he managed the rose department at Roger's Gardens. He later became a consultant "Rosarino" for the American Rose Society. He has authored two books on the care of roses, including *Coastal Roses: Selection and Care for Southern California*. He lived in Los Alamitos, California, for 35 years. When his wife passed, he moved into the Frank Residences.

A Freeway Through the Street

When I was a young boy in Richmond, Virginia, I did not get along with my parents and could not wait until I was old enough to leave. Many years later, my wife picked up the phone and cried. I said, "What's wrong?" and she said my mother had died. All I said was, "Too bad!"

A few years after that I was back in Richmond and thought I would drive by my old house. It wasn't there anymore; they had built a freeway through the street. I thought I would call my mother and tell her. But then a tear dropped from my eye. I realized she was dead.

In the Navy

When I was 18 years old and in the Navy, I was stationed in Virginia at Oceana Naval Air Station, in Security. I was on Gate Watches. I had never shot a gun before, but had to carry a loaded .45. They showed me how to use it—if someone attacked at the gate, I was to shoot him in the stomach because the head moves and is harder to hit. The .45 will blow his stomach out. All that made me sick as hell, but I served my country and got an honorable discharge with no great war stories to tell.

Old Lady Nature

Nature is my education, work, and my life. Mother Nature was on Earth before Adam and Eve and the other original species. But humans have not been kind to her. They destroyed the beautiful forests and a lot of land so they could build what humans wanted. Mother Nature doesn't take this lying down. She reacts with force, and starts the Great War of Wars. She attacks back with horrific earthquakes and devastating hurricanes. Don't mess with Old Lady Nature—she'll still be here when humans kill themselves off with dissent and war.

A Great Man

When my grandfather arrived in this country from Lithuania at age 17, he enlisted in the Army. He said his name was Peter Span. I don't think there are any Peter Spans in Lithuanian phone books. He made the Army his career, which gained him his citizenship. He served with "Teddy Bear" Roosevelt in the Spanish American War in Cuba. My grandfather was wounded, with shrapnel in his head, but refused to go back to the States for treatment because he didn't want a medical discharge—he wanted to stay in the Army. When he married my grandmother, he retired from the Army. They had three kids—my father, his brother and sister. My grandfather was about six feet tall and never fat, even in later years. He was always in military shape. He died when he was 78 years old, and still looked like he could beat up anybody in the room. I miss him to this day.

Richmond, Virginia, 1942

When I was about 10 years old, I used to walk to the Grand Theatre on Broad Street. I'd go up to the counter to buy a ticket and dig into my pocket for the 12 cents to get in. Once, a soldier said he would buy my ticket, but I found my money. The Grand Theatre played Westerns along with about six cartoons and a serial. They sold popcorn in the lobby for 10 cents, and that was how I spent my Saturday afternoons.

Now that I am 91, I still think of those afternoons. I watch TV, and all I see is the war in Ukraine, crime, and Donald Trump. I wish I was 10 again, when life was sweet and easy, and I watched Johnny Mack Brown, Gene Autry, Roy Rogers, and those weekly serials.

Michael Thaler

Born 1934 near Lviv, presently Western Ukraine. Of approximately 4,000 Jews in the town, 130 survived the Holocaust, including Michael Thaler's parents and himself. He spent three and a half years in a displaced persons camp, emigrated to Toronto, graduated from the University of Toronto School of Medicine. He finished postgraduate training, then served as professor of pediatrics and chief of pediatric gastroenterology at UCSF for 34 years and adjunct professor of history at UC Santa Cruz for 11 years. Michael married Libby in 1966; they have two children and five grandchildren.

Birthplace

The room overlooked a lumberyard that stretched from my grandfather's house, where we lived, to where Rina lived. Rina and I were about four years old, and she was my girlfriend. She was the only child my age on the entire block, and the lumberyard stretched from the street between our houses to a fast-flowing rivulet, a creek with steep banks, which was crossed on a narrow wooden bridge by a road that led up to our large blue pond, where we swam in the summer heat.

Rina and I played hide-and-seek among the high stacks of lumber and often slid down the embankment into the clear cold water, getting our shoes wet and our clothes dirty.

My mother said, "If you promise never to go near that creek, I'll let you go out into the lumberyard. If you don't, you'll never see Rina again."

And the war broke out, and I never saw Rina. I never saw her again.

About two years ago, for a special birthday, my daughter and son said, "We got a birthday present for you. We're going to take you back to the town where you were born in eastern Poland," in what is now Western Ukraine.

We all went back together, and the place where I was born, in my grandfather's house, of course had been razed to the ground by the Germans. And now there was nothing but a neglected park or street. And I said, "Here I was born, on that particular corner, and the street is still named the same as it was before. This was the street, and that's where I was born, that very spot." And they said, "How can you be so sure?" And I said, "Because there was a lumberyard, and in the back, a creek." And my son said, "Well, in that case, let's go over and see if there's a creek."

So we walked and sure enough, there's a little bridge, and a creek.

Just as there had been 81 years ago.

My German Lessons

At the end of World War II, my parents and I found ourselves among other survivors of the Holocaust in a displaced persons camp near Linz, the capital of Upper Austria—and incidentally Hitler's hometown. Father had been elected treasurer of the committee that governed the camp, and Mother helped with retraining the younger women for employment; I was left free to hang out with a handful of other unsupervised children in the camp.

This ideal arrangement (from my perspective) lasted for more than a year. Days after my bar mitzvah in the camp recreation barrack, Father confronted me: "As far as I can tell, you have nothing to do all day but play ping-pong in the rec hall or soccer with a *schmatta* ball in the street. Soon you'll turn into a hooligan." "What's a hooligan?" I countered, to change the subject. Next morning, Mother dressed me in my Sabbath outfit—white shirt, tie, long pants, polished black shoes. I asked her what's up, and Father cut in, peering closely at me over the top of his glasses.

"Instead of going to the office today, I've made other arrangements. I'm taking you to a school in the city." Having never attended school, I was intimidated, but as a budding hooligan, I didn't let on how I felt.

We got off the bus in front of an ancient three-story stone edifice with *Realschule* carved above the entrance over the trace of a recently removed swastika. Father and I mounted the wide spiraling stairs to the top floor, and entered a large, well-lighted room lined with bookshelves that rose to the ceiling. A gray-haired man emerged from behind a massive desk and smiled at us under an enormous mustache that made him look like Kaiser Franz Joseph in my stamp collection. He and my father spoke in German, so I understood not a word. At last, they shook hands and we left. "You are now enrolled as a *Gastschüler*, a guest student," Father announced as we walked out of the building. "Just sit in the back, keep your ears open and your mouth shut, and you will begin to understand what's going on." "But I don't speak German," I pleaded. Father nodded. "Don't worry. The principal arranged a tutor who will give you lessons in German twice a week. The tutor was once a top Nazi, so they can't employ him officially, but the principal assured me he's an excellent teacher."

The tutor and I met Tuesdays and Thursdays in an abandoned chemistry lab. We perched on high stools and leaned against lab benches with dusty black Formica tops. He was younger than Father, very elegant and formal. "Every Tuesday you will hand in a *Komposition*, which I will correct in red ink and give you a grade on Thursday," he enunciated slowly in German, which I even more slowly deconstructed into my primitive Yiddish. After an hour with my Nazi, I proceeded to an assigned class and sat in the back, attracting over-the-shoulder glances from curious boys. This went on for three months; each week my German improved and I was beginning to match the students' faces with their names. But my *Komposition* bled red ink and earned grades of "*nicht genügend* (unsatisfactory)." Finally came a Thursday when there was less red ink, and a single word below the text: "*genügend.*" "Does this mean we can stop the lessons?" I asked. He nodded. "*Sehr genügend!* (Very satisfactory!)," I exclaimed, and climbed down from my perch. He wagged a finger at me. "You don't understand. This is truly a great day for you. *Kommen Sie mit!* (Come along!)"

We went down the winding stair to a dank cellar. The tutor turned on a naked bulb encased in cobwebs. Shelves bearing mildewed volumes of student records, each denoted with a year on its spine, ran along the rough-hewn stone foundation of the building. The tutor pulled out a tome with "1904" on its spine. "*Da! Lesen Sie!* (Here! Read!)" He pointed with the red-ink-stained finger to an entry on a moldy, yellowed page. "*Adolf Hitler, Deutsche Sprache, Nicht Genügend*," I read. "Congratulations," he said, and almost imperceptibly clicked his heels. "Today, your German is superior to the Führer's!"

The next Tuesday morning, I slept in. When my bewildered mother woke me up, I announced, "I don't need to go to that school anymore. My German is better than Hitler's!"

Janet Underwood

Janet Underwood lived in New York until her late 20s, when she moved to California, where her boyfriend at the time lived. She was a teacher of the deaf and learning disabled for 30-plus years.

Middle Name

My name is Janet. When I was born, my name was Janet B. Shapiro. As I grew up, I often asked my mother what the "B" stood for. She said, "Oh, it could be anything—Beth, Betty, or whatever." I asked why she gave me an initial and not a full name. She didn't have an answer.

"Call yourself whatever you want," she said. "Beatrice is nice," she said.

"But why didn't you give me a name?" I would ask. She could never reply except to say B. would help to identify me if there was another Janet Shapiro.

I just always said my name was Janet B. Shapiro.

Now I ask you—how hard would it have been to give me a name instead of only an initial?

Koko and Me

What does one talk about with a gorilla? What does a gorilla think and dream? These questions were on my mind during my first encounter with Koko the gorilla. She sat in her large cage on a trailer platform, cradling her pet, a kitten she named All Ball, as she fiddled with a piece of cloth in her hands. It was apparent from the moment we met that Koko wanted to involve me in play. She gently pushed the cloth through the bars of the cage three or four times to get me to pull the cloth toward me and out of the cage. When I engaged in this game, Koko suddenly yanked the cloth with such force that my face was thrown against the bars. That first day, it was the human who had learned a lesson. Koko's playfulness was part of her impressive ability to manipulate and control the action.

One day I threw Koko a treat. It looked like it fell in the toilet. Koko peered in the toilet and at me repeatedly, so I threw her a second piece.

She immediately caught it and ate it. Then she retrieved the first piece that was obscured from my sight. So, she tricked me!

My work with Koko came about when I happened to hear a televised interview with Penny Patterson, who described her work teaching sign language to a female gorilla. Koko had been a baby when Penny began her research as a graduate student at Stanford. The work continued after Penny received her degree and took Koko into her home. Eventually, Penny taught the young gorilla over 1,500 words. During the interview, Penny called for applicants to assist with this work. I was employed as a teacher of sign language to deaf people at the time. I called Penny and was accepted on the spot as a volunteer. I would leave my teaching job early in the afternoon several times a week, drive 45 minutes to Koko's abode in Palo Alto, and sign back and forth with her for three hours. My job was to stimulate conversation with the gorilla and record the responses she signed back to me in GSL (Gorilla Sign Language) as Patterson labeled it.

Koko knew how to use language when she felt like it. Her name for her beloved All Ball neatly described the appearance of this tailless feline breed when curled up into a furry globe. The huge gorilla carried All Ball with her everywhere, handling the delicate kitten with extreme gentleness and affection. So, what does a human say to a gorilla? Whatever the gorilla wishes to hear. What does a gorilla think and dream about? Koko, the female gorilla, thought she was the mother of a child and dreamed the child's name was All Ball.

§

Community Living Campaign: Cayuga Connectors

Elina Adams

After retiring from teaching kindergarten in Houston, Texas, Elina Adams moved to San Francisco in 2015 with her sister Beth Arnaoot. Elina and Beth enjoyed the City Guides Library Tours, music events, neighborhood festivals, and speakers at the Jewish Community Center. When the pandemic came, Elina and Beth discovered the Zoom writing classes sponsored by the Community Living Campaign, including Litquake's Wednesday night class. Thank you, Litquake and CLC.

Rant

I'm tired of shoplifting in San Francisco.
Watching a handsome young man grabbing
all the large display boxes of M&M's at Walgreens
Then seeing him stuff them
in his large black backpack
at the corner of Polk and California.
No M&M's for sister Beth,
No M&M's for sister Liny.
Now so many things are locked up at Walgreens.
I have to call a clerk to unlock the shampoo.
I spend so much time waiting for that clerk.
I'm tired of shoplifting in San Francisco.

Jane Alexander

Jane Alexander's master's degree looked at creativity from the perspectives of psychology, sociology, philosophy, and art. She worked as an art and drama therapist, and after her retirement, focused on her own visual art, combining photography and painting. It wasn't until learning became available online, due to the pandemic, that she began writing. With the prompts offered in CLC and Litquake classes, she has written about both her history and her ongoing questions about life and the way the mind works.

The Fall

Fall in New York City, orange and yellow; horseback riding in Central Park on Amherst. I could have been a park ranger but the economy fell, the money tree fell down. The income fell away in the city budget and so I left to find horses in Sonoma. And when the Sonoma budget fell in 1979, I was no longer an art and drama therapist, to save the county money.

I fell off a horse the first year or so of lessons in Forest Park. I was five years old and didn't care, I wasn't hurt, it was a rite of passage, and I passed. It made me stronger and more confident. I was always confident to go on to the next opportunity, from being a therapist to becoming a photographer. Then falling from that into being a graphic designer. Once I fell into unemployment and had to clean my friend's house to pay my rent. I also fell so low that I worked for a guy who had me paste receipts from restaurants and coffee shops into a notebook to prove his business expenses... even receipts for 49 cents. I was puzzled and repelled by him for being like that.

My aunt, disciplined and organized, kept receipts in a file. I was curious because she was retired. I guess she wanted to make sure stores hadn't overcharged her. In my mind, a waste of time. I have never been and will never be that organized person. Sometimes I am sorry that I am in chaos in my home and paperwork and don't get things done, but then I think, Who cares?

In Central Park, cherry trees with pink blossoms lined the jogging path. Their petals fell. When there was still a stable in New York, I found places to canter and sometimes gallop. My friend fell off Amherst when she asked me to let her ride him, my favorite horse. Amherst loved me, as I loved him. We rode together for about a year, sometimes three or four times a week. He was sold, and I wish I could have bought him myself and taken him to Sonoma. Now I live in San Francisco, where there are no defined seasons, no oranges of fall.

Beth Arnaoot

Beth Arnaoot grew up the oldest of five children in the suburbs, the daughter of an oil company executive in the age of "I've been moved..." A homemaker with three delightful children, she volunteered in schools, churches, and occasionally, hospitals. She discovered the pleasures of writing in her 70s through Community Living Campaign.

Ode to Hopscotch

Feline, clawed,
rough-tongued, flashing movement.
Black, shiny in the sun, invisible in the night
  when I stomp on your tail.
Observant, seeing tiny flies in the air,
leaping, catapulting.
Warm, bringing comfort
to whichever Mom needs it.
Egyptians worshiped your kin,
Who protected precious grain.
Food for now and food for the future.
The ignorant hated you
Seeing your face as devilish
A hiding place for witches.
Bird lovers avoided you
Seeing your hunting nature as vicious
Harming their feathered friends.
You have brought food
Small creatures killed to fill the larder
Unappreciated by your human family.
You have allowed us to love you
Your warm body pulling the need to protect

To nurture, to love
Our non-human child.

Doris Beers

Doris Beers is a 70-year-old poet who transplanted from Philadelphia in 1984. As a side hustle, she spent 25 years working in San Francisco's tech sector, noting its rises and falls. She has given up long walks on the beach (and sidewalk) in the face of several serious diagnoses. She continues to investigate what this sudden change may mean.

Just Three Knocks

Just three knocks
Plain, no special rhythm
I know no one is there

The first time
I dream of padding barefoot through the dark house
Listening and watching
Hoping for and against an answer

I learned to navigate my dreams
Years ago
I woke again and again into the same horror
Until I could force myself to speak or scream

The knocks strike dread
Each time
Like portents in a Victorian novel
I sit motionless
Not daring to breathe
Assuming I am awake

What if I've got it wrong

How death happens?
If I often cannot tell
Whether I'm awake or asleep
How will I know
When the enemy in my bones
Has done its worst
Or best?

The Wrong Journey

This apparently auspicious beginning
Has become a disorienting stutter step.
An enterprise not started well is bound to fail.
This will fail.
I need it to fail more slowly
With fewer stops and starts
Than others I have held watch over.
And now I hover at a threshold.
I fret that my seer and hers both
Declaimed the deadly 10-year promise.
It hangs like a challenge to the liminal gods.
Can I be alert and open, try for trusting or wise?
Each day brings another nugget of maybe for my net
That I must trade for small, spangled measures of hope.
Optimism is worth a planetary itch.
I know how this ends. That is not in question.
Just the how and the when and how hard the
    in-between.

After Surgery

Does it loosen, my winding cloth?
Its tight embrace
Promised to hold me safe
After the worst happened.
After the deadly diagnoses
One after another.
Under the rough linen
I am slippery clean
Washed by devoted hands
Anointed with stinging
Purifying oils.
My skin, this time, has broken down.

What would it be to breathe again
Smoothly, without paroxysm?
Do I taste the heavy metal
Of a coin in my mouth
Feel the mild pressure
Of tape on my eyelids?
What would it be
To feel warm blood
Rush to my fingertips again?

How could I leave my cloth?
Its grip holds me in place.
My flesh stays on my bones,
Unlike last time.
My winding cloth, does it loosen?
As I rest, enclosed, do I dream?
Are these the last flashes of unrelenting nerves
Fighting still for clarity?

I prefer vague uncertainty.
My ghost-cold fingers
Tug the shroud close
Like a winter cloak
And wait for other hands
To free me.

Sunday after Midnight

I turn away from the old poets tonight
(I miss the rain.)
But one blunt word
In one short stanza
Reminds me
(I miss the fog and the damp dirt.)
Of something buried deep
Of the joyous abandon
Of stepping into the rain
Face to the sky
Drenched
Choosing to be one
With the cool and damp.
Not to show anyone that I am
Fun
Or any of the other ways men say
Available
Or
Not marriage material
Though both are right
But even in my married mother days
That step into the wild

Was bliss and bliss just for me
I did not care
If anyone joined in
I preferred no audience
No one going along to
Try a taste of
Free or silly
Or however they read the text.
I miss
The kidney-cutting wind
At the base
Of the city's
Too tall too square
Towers
In the too soon dusk
Sliding in from the hills
And the sea
Multiplied and aimed
Slamming the unwary
Staggered by its force
Struggling
To the train, to the bus, home.
I miss the rain
My rain

My enveloping fog
My kidney cutting wind
My hands full of dark wet dirt
Like the moon,
That once lit up my room, improbably,
At 5 am, in winter.

Naomi Cooper

Naomi Cooper grew up in Savannah, Georgia, and earned a master's degree in Hispanic Literature at Indiana University. In San Francisco, she worked as a Kelly Girl, house cleaner, child-care provider, clairvoyant reader, and teacher in the public schools. Now retired, she's been published in *Cayuga Connections, Forum, Haight Ashbury Literary Journal*, and *Quarantine Fiction.*

Ode to the Upstairs Neighbor Dog

The little dachshund,
not too long grown
out of puppyhood,
lives with the old woman's
upstairs neighbors.
They keep his red-brown fur
very clean, like fall leaves,
just finished with a bath of rain.
So stretched out, low to the ground,
he sounds loud as a little buffalo,
racing along the third floor hallway,
thudding out a heartbeat
for the building.

Still, he's adaptable enough
to synchronize his stubby legs
to a crone's slow pace,
when accompanying the old woman
for their evening constitutional.
He smiles at passersby,
who smile back,
fondle his big dangly ears.

One night the old woman dreams
of him, and his eyes look human,
but kinder than human,
as though in understanding
of how his vitality stirs
her own faithfulness with life.
The neighbors call
this good companion
Copper Kettle,
since he boils
with
such
bright
joy.

Love Song Riding

The sky goes pink and gold. Sun, just rising,
imprints pale rose shadows upon the sand.
Everything feels quiet.
Even seagulls, milling around the seawall,
have not yet begun their squawking.
We ride an appaloosa,
who loves her leisurely pace, loves us,
moves carefully, wanting to prevent any falls.
I hold onto you, press forward,
balanced at your back.
The air smells clean, rinsed with light and salt
from waves dissolved
into scrims of lace against the shore.
And this water lapping,
the mare's muted clopping hooves,
you and I breathing together,
sometimes even yawning in time,
make graceful pleats
of sound that fan out along the beach,
then open further
toward the warm day, which will soon unfold,
after dawn's soft chill is done.

Water

Mountain stream
gathers light,
like fast-moving
liquid clouds,
and wanting
this wild flow
for just a moment,
you sit still on the bank—
surrender, become
the stream, returned
to presence,
rushing sweet spirit of water.
And in this
small space,
there gushes
trickery, enchantment,
maybe truth
of joy
that can be washed
clean from time,
with all fear
rippled away.

Surrender

After loss, the heart gets encased with cold,
a kind of easing,
configurations of detachment, solitude,
comforting snowy gleaming,
almost like forgiveness.
So then if time should bring new company,
warmth encountering winter snowfall,
fear will also
reveal its trembling self, because
what first manifests as hope
may take turn, spiraling toward unexpected grief.
And you know that
one of the bravest things
a human being can do
is allowing snow to change, take penetration,
its pristine whiteness reflecting vivid colors,
transparency of need.
An amazement how every day
surprise and night,
people take this risk
of surrendering impermeability, becoming
so gorgeous in their courage.

Grace D'Anca

Minnesota native Grace D'Anca came to San Francisco in the mid-sixties. She performed with small theater and improv dance ensembles, worked 45 years as a creative arts therapist with children, youth, and adults, and collaborated with community groups to create murals, mosaics installations, and cultural events in the Excelsior District. Retired now, she is writing, making art, participating in theater pieces, and dancing with the mirror.

I Wanted to Know How It Would End

for Sophia/Kate

It's a big house now with too many rooms for two.
How did they end up in a nascent suburb
in the first house built on open land.

He from a flat above a cigar store commuters stormed
every weekday morning, she
from a tidy little house with a screen porch
where her mother made May altars and prayed
sorrowful mysteries of the rosary during Lent.

She can only reach the bottom shelf.
Her crooked spine will not allow her to drag a chair
to reach for tins of dreams on the second shelf.
She goes without now. Puts on her red rimmed glasses
so she won't step on the shards of hope
that fell on thick blue carpet when he died.

Queen Casey

She used to sing
off-key, *forte*
some silly song
we were surprised
she knew.

She used to sing in front
of the lace curtains
overlooking the parking lot
and the leaning eucalyptus tree
I feared would collapse the house
that El Niño.

She used to sing *fortissimo*
in her red shirt with pastel hearts
from Goodwill, always
wrinkled.

She was four
and it didn't matter
then.

Something Sometimes

for Baga Jim

Something dropped in the kitchen this morning.
Even the cat was startled. And she never met you.
We bolted out the covers.
Looked in all the rooms, found
nothing untoward. It must have been next door.
I'm reluctant to think you will come back
from wherever you are now.
It wouldn't be like you.
You knew it was time to go.
Someone said *stay with the body*
at the moment of death
when the spirit is the strongest. I stayed
to make sure you were really gone.
You agonized about being stuck
alive with no voice to say so.
You would have liked
the young men who carried you out
under darkness, unseen
by neighbors. I stay busy,
opportunities materializing
like venetian blinds flicking open.

It’s not sad so much
as empty. An emotional North
and South Dakota. A flat line to
where? People say it gets better. So what
who needs all this space? Sometimes
I cry during the cooldown song
at Wednesday Zumba.

If We Don't Speak

If we don't speak
can we learn to dance
and drum

if we don't see can we read
the faces across the aisle
eyes only, imagine

their stories, rooms,
burdens, thoughts scalding
their blood as we lurch

through the jangled mess of desire
and despair at the transfer
to the next stop

if we don't listen
can we learn to breathe
the tumult across the aisle
warm in layers of privilege
without struggle, born
safe from ever having to walk

barefoot on hot asphalt
over broken glass
to dance and drum?

Helen Dannenberg

Helen Dannenberg, from old-fashioned Brooklyn, was a dance major at School of the Performing Arts, after performing with the Merry-Go-Rounders. In California, she performed and taught for Margaret Jenkins. That was followed by 24 years working in long-term care. Retirement: wonderful classes in writing, visual arts, theater including Cosmic Elders Theatre Ensemble. Writing and readings: published in San Francisco City College's *Forum* magazine, the *Noe Valley Voice*, the *Community Living Campaign Journal*, and *OWL Older Writers Laboratory*. Thank you, Litquake!

Hello New Poetry

A dark green cover, the title in dull gold:
The New Poetry: An Anthology of Twentieth-
Century Verse in English.
A thick book, 775 pages,
including biographical notes.
The text up to p. 686, notes starting p. 687.

I don't associate my father with poetry
or any other reading. Vaguely
I remember hearing something
about my parents meeting
when he was selling books.
Is that true?
The book is in good condition.
The inscription:

To Felice
With great affection
Eli
Dec 25, 1935

Very proper, very respectful.

The book, the book is the frame.
When I knew my father
he was too tired from working to read,
except the *New York Times* on Sunday.
We would watch television
downstairs in the living room
while my mother was upstairs
in the bedroom, reading.
I have my mother's books—many falling to shreds.
I can't bear to part with them.
I never looked at this book when it was housed
  in the brown bookcase in our living room.
And now, now I want it to tell me:
Was it there when my parents met?
What was he—a tailor—doing selling books?
Did Felice happen to arrive at the table where
Eli was selling books?
Did she ask about the books?
Hello, she says.
Can you tell me the price of this one here,
and that one there?
He looks up the prices, tells her.
They continue the conversation.

A Plan

Follow it.
Too much now
  to think of
too much
  to understand
too much
  to fix.
I have to learn
a use, a purpose for memories
so they don't swallow me,
tear at me, make my heart hurt.

(*Er raist shtiker fun mir*:
  He tears pieces from me—Yiddish)
Go away.

Absorb it.
Keep a protective barrier of soft cloth
to be removed only when feeling
strong enough.

Eureka: I Found It

Class—dance class—yay!
What I want to do—where I want to be
I have found classes I like.
Coming from New York, who knew?
What would I find?
Would it be anything I could respect?
This is good. This is the real deal.
I give it my stamp of approval.
I get warmed up.
Serious—modern dance
I am a serious modern dancer.
What else am I?

The class starts. Such a comfort to slide in.
All's right with the world.
We are in the studio
Leotards, tights, maybe sweaters
We mill around.
The teacher at the front,
We arrange ourselves.
I have agreed with the teacher
That I will stand in front

because I don't remember combinations well.
I won't depend on anyone else.
I'll make my own mistakes.
Cunningham technique—better here than in
The cold Cunningham studio in New York.
I was so cold there, didn't last long.

Class repeats daily
Taking or teaching—
Dependable.

Paco Lorenzo Melgar

Paco Melgar was born and raised in Manila. Until recently, he was an intern at California Academy of Sciences through Arc San Francisco. He enjoyed hosting groups of schoolchildren with their chaperones, letting them into the Planetarium, Rainforest, and Earthquake exhibitions, and giving safety instructions. His focus is children's science education.

Occasion

My first cousin's 25th silver wedding anniversary was the occasion. I can't deny wearing formal dress whenever there is an in-person event. We have to respect the couple. The necktie is highly recommended. I love the entertainment—music and dance and piano. I felt compassion that people were exposed to Covid in a public setting. My aunt and I self-quarantined for three days.

"Best of" New Year's List

The alarm clock goes off
when the new year officially begins
New Year's resolutions, fireworks displays
Making new acquaintances
New beginnings, fresh footprints
A blank sheet of paper
Making promises, having new clothes,
new opportunities.

Joe Ochab

Primarily a prose writer, Joe Ochab lives in San Francisco, where he has participated in Litquake and other elder writing groups/classes since 2019. In retirement, Joe often writes about his passion for the arts, about gardening, and his experiences as a federal park ranger, forester, and outdoor recreational planner.

Dancing with the "You" and the "I" in a Duet of Silent Conversation

You peer into the room with more than mild anticipation. Then perhaps you take a deep breath and confidently walk in, half hiding your true feelings and state of mind. You hope no one will notice that you are a relative newcomer to the art or are "rusty" since you have not kept up with it.

You seriously want to fit in and do well in this class. It's a strong human desire—something you've felt before when facing kinetic and memory challenges. But after all, it's just a college gym—less intimidating than a club, you remind yourself. You tell yourself to relax; there are no dire consequences if you fail to dance well, rhetorically fall on your face, happen to embarrass yourself, or perhaps receive disapproving looks. "*I'm okay.* No big deal, be more positive… lighten up!" you tell yourself.

You spot someone who appears to be the dance instructor talking to other neophytes—or perhaps more advanced students. You don't know what their level of dance training and competency truly is, much less their expectations for the students. But there are those around the room with smiling as well as pensive faces. Like you, they may have the jitters—maybe not perspiring in body but overcharged in their minds and emotions, same as you are! You decide to be cool and friendly, but not overly so. You look around the room again for any familiar or approachable faces.

When the opportunity arises, you approach the dance instructor, say hello, and give them your name. They greet you: "Welcome! You look somewhat familiar! Have you taken social dance classes here before?" You reply and your name is checked off their registration list. The instructor seems personable and empathetic—likely very competent. You fervently hope that their instructional pace is not based on the skill level displayed by the majority of students present. Yet you don't wish to be bored and held back either. You are serious about improving your ballroom dancing!

A few of the students—mainly couples—are dancing on their own to the tunes and dance styles of the recorded music overhead. "Oh, I forgot the steps to that one!" you tell yourself. You view their dancing with fascination, curiosity, and perhaps envy. Soon, you begin instead to view their dancing with interest and as a way to recall steps that you once thought you'd mastered but for which you now draw a blank. So you note their steps and hope the music jogs your memory.

You see a face or two in the crowd that you recall meeting in a former dance class or club. That dissipates much of the discomfort and angst that's been overtaking you. You approach and re-introduce yourself. You ask someone who is not coupled at the moment to "practice dance" to the music. They happily oblige and you put away your insecurities out of curiosity, attraction, and perhaps a desire to let go and live in the moment!

At this stage, you lighten up a little and ask your accommodating partner a few questions about themselves and perhaps compliment them on their dancing. You may even manage to get them to smile. You ask their first name but soon forget it during dancing with them. Curiosity then overtakes you and you ask where they go dancing or practice dancing. You're tempted to suggest you both go dancing outside of class sometime. But you don't want to appear too bold or off-putting, so you decide to defer that offer or suggestion to another time.

All of it is part of "the dance"—the social interaction that ebbs and flows in many ways. As the initial music ends and the instructor announces the beginning of the class, you thank your partner. And you even hope you remember their name when you dance with them again—perhaps later during the class as the instructor firmly but sweetly announces: "Change partners, please!"

Lee Ellen Shoemaker

Lee Ellen Shoemaker taught photography and digital media at San Francisco City College. In her mid-50s, she became the Tunnel Singer, an ambient musician. When spasmodic dysphonia, a movement disorder, disabled Lee Ellen's voice, she evolved journal writing into personal narrative and fiction writing. Her turbulent early life and persistent curiosity inspire stories and poems, and Litquake's classes have helped her shape and develop her writing skills. Writing offers the peace and fulfillment once provided by creating music.

Bunker Hill Air Force Base, Summer 1957

We park at the end of the runway
under star-spattered skies
we wait we talk
we make out
smoke cigarettes
hum to the radio turned low
A mild whine joins in
We leave the car.
A barely visible KC 135 grows as it thunders forth
Its whine becomes ear-shattering
Black emissions spew
The Stratotanker heaves up
The powerful shriek judders our bones
We scream
    We hug
        We jump up and down
            We stop.
The air crackles and fizzes
Static electricity lifts every hair
Crickets chirp. Mosquitoes sing.
We climb in the car to avoid their bite.
We wait.

Summer Games

I.

My little brother Buddy and I roamed our neighborhood, sifting through trash piled in the incinerators behind houses. Curious about what people threw away we always hoped to find something we could use or fix or play with. We also knocked on back doors and asked for empty pop bottles. We could return them to the drugstore for two cents apiece. If we collected five empties, we could each buy a strawberry ice cream cone for a nickel or a grape popsicle.

Together, we trudged down alleys, Buddy pulling his red Radio Flyer wagon until he got too tired to walk, then I pulled him. We searched for anything worn out or torn up that contained pretty colors or missing parts. We named the objects we knew and discussed the possible use of those interesting items we couldn't identify. We especially liked empty boxes, broken things we might be able to fix, and empty tin cans with the labels still on.

II.

We once made a funhouse in the garage. We nailed cardboard over the windows to make it dark. We put chunks of wood, mounds of rags, and various junk on the garage floor to make a bumpy path for Buddy's wagon. We charged neighbor kids five cents apiece to pull them around in the wagon in the dark, yanking them over bumps and making ghostly moans and frightening screams all the while. It was a modest financial success.

III.

Summer evenings, in the schoolyard several houses away, we played ditch 'em, a game of hide-and-seek. A few kids who played softball until it got too dark joined in. We used "one potato, two potato, three potato four…" to determine who would be "it" to begin. The big sycamore tree marked "home," and the edges of the schoolyard, out of bounds. The last player found became the winner. Once Buddy won by hiding on the third floor of the school's outside wrought-iron fire escape. No one expected such a little kid to climb way up there. I was afraid to. After that, he always hid there. After a few times telling him that it was out of bounds we just let him go there. He wouldn't come down until everyone else was found.

Sometimes, if enough kids had bikes with them, we played ditch 'em on bikes. We'd decide which streets marked the edge of fair territory for bike ditch 'em. Someone always "forgot" and hid too far away. No one saw them until well after "Outy outy all in free" was called to end the game.

IV.

The street we lived on had brick sidewalks, no good for roller skating. We carried our skates with the straps buckled together, slung over our shoulder. Everyone wore a skate key on a lanyard around their neck to tighten the clamps. If we arrived at the paved schoolyard basketball court before any basketball players arrived, we sat on the benches made from bark-covered logs to fasten our skates to the soles of our shoes.

If two or three boys were already practicing dribbling and shooting baskets at one end of the cement court, we would skate on the other end. If enough boys showed up to make two teams, we knew they would chase us off if we didn't automatically yield to them.

V.

After the city of Kokomo replaced some of the brick sidewalks with cement, Buddy and I discovered newly paved sidewalks just three blocks from our house. These unbelievably smooth sidewalks contained Silicarb, a combination of silicon and carbon that sparkles in sunlight. We skated so fast we created a vortex of cool air around us. We were no longer hot, poor, fatherless children. We were falcons, soaring over diamonds.

Greg Taylor (aka Horehound Stillpoint)

Greg Taylor is a writer, worker, and retired waiter in San Francisco, performing and publishing poetry as Horehound Stillpoint. He loves opera, theater, rock 'n' roll, walking, swimming, doing Qigong, studying Kadam Buddhism, reading, sharing poetry at open mics (hey, Labyrinth buddies!), writing workshops (ditto!), gay bars, movies, trees, the Moon, the San Francisco Symphony, and maybe most of all, friends.

I Was Told by Forces I Do Not Understand to Come Share This Exact Thing with You

also known as The Crowd Sighs "Uh, Oh," Groans, Eyerolls, Etc. And So, Here Goes Nothing

I do not understand why
I keep trying to ruin my life
Ruin my relationships
Ruin my finances
Ruin my ability to swallow in a way
  that will nourish
Something / Anything
(God, Todd, thank you for the years)
But the sky took me aback today
I kept seeing a dragon
Long sultry neck
Wide open ripped and ripping wings
The clouds wrestled and there was a rustle
Though there was no breeze
Blue sky wispy fairy streaking arabesques
Did you see it yesterday?
A moonwake rumbled up
from the dragon in my spirit
Burying everything

And denying it all   forever
This big   NO
I am ready to leave behind
Some mystical rainbreak
No   No   No   No   No   No
Greg! Stop ruining your life
Plainspoken, undeniably wise undeniably
loving advice
From Beth and Liny: Zoom pals from the
Litquake Elder Writers Group
Including Paco, MG, Grace, Helen, Lee Ellen,
Joe, Doris, Roger
and Naomi
(And I'm not the only one who misses Jane)
Not to mention the teachers
The love would be un e n d i n g
Not to mention the gratitude
One might call infinite
There's your proof   [see above]   and
There's your solution   [see below]
100%

He Sang "Jamaica Farewell" to Us All

Mom, Dad, my sister Sherry and I,
 at the World's Fair in 1963
  standing in the longest line ever that day
10,000 people (total guess)
 in Escher-like confabulation
Erector Set-looking spans, bridges,
 underpasses, overpasses
People people everywhere utterly silent because

 Harry Belafonte was singing
  "Jamaica Farewell"

And he had just delivered that immortal line
I had to leave a little girl in Kingston Town
For maybe the third time, after which
—he took a long dramatic pause
 which just about broke everybody's heart

Still shocking—even now—to have to admit
 I yelled out: *Why?*
My little boy voice so loud, everybody heard
 including Mr. Belafonte

I swear I thought my big sister might murder
me on the spot
Really who would have blamed her?
I didn't mean to do it, I just had to ask

Well, God Bless Harry Belafonte
He chuckled for a second or two
Before he carried on singing beautifully as ever
What a man, what a voice, what a spirit
Even my sister had to forgive me
In light of his breathtaking
generosity

Lucky Son of a Bundle of Nerves

I like feeling healthy, wealthy, strong, and safe
    —good luck with *that* in 2023—
Luckily, just getting outdoors feels Heavenly
—my little studio: home of so much poetry
    and so little cleaning—
Seeing a full moon, half moon, silver crescent
I call that a red letter day!
You can't imagine my happiness at the San
    Francisco Ballet
Giselle, my first full-on Romantic ballet and I
    love love loved it
Despite being a die-hard, decrepit, and fading
    heavy-metal-kid
    gay punk rocker, poet, and Buddhist
I fell in love with the San Francisco Symphony in 2022
Who wouldn't with Prokofiev, Gershwin,
    Bartók, and Sibelius
Esa-Pekka Salonen and Yuja Wang
    bringing all their muscle and magic to bear
I've loved the San Francisco Opera since 1991
    Eugene Onegin, Orpheus and Eurydice,

revelations this year
plus my favorite *Traviata ev-ver*
The Fillmore, Warfield, Masonic Auditorium
(Iggy Pop is coming!)
Poetry and open mics
Books from the library, books from friends,
books by friends
Friends!
Teachers of writing, teachers of Buddhism, of
Vedas, and Qigong
Where would I be without teachers? Not here
Trees, trees, and more trees
Every tree I go by, I lean toward
I nod and silently say:

Tayatha Om
Bekhadze Bekhadze Maha Bekhadze
Randzaya Samugate Soha

Trying to plant a seed of Medicine Buddha's blessings
The paintings on my walls from a lifetime ago
when Michael was still alive (*no tears, please*)
Oh, I am a lucky son of a bundle of nerves and
potentiality

This is what it takes to get one tragic gloomy-
doomy freak
from 1952 to 2023
A thousand apologies would not be enough
for the life I've led
And one would be too many
Residing now—as I do—at the level of the heart
Where the softest gratitude grows

If I Die Tonight, at Least … This

Been obsessing about angel food cake lately
Not so surprising, considering
I just saw my own private demon
Head to head he got in my face
Up or down on my level
Blazing red eyes, jagged brown teeth
Obviously evil grin
Chased me out of a home
Down the sidewalk in the wrong direction
Made three bus drivers sail right past me
He could make a person run and still not get
 anywhere
His eyes said "I own you"
His laugh said "I'll see you"
But in the morning he had faded back to
 wherever
He saw who was on my walls
Who was in my heart
Who was at my crown
Buddha Mother Tara, Medicine Buddha,
 Avalokitashvara
 in whose presence a demon can only bow

and blanch
and be reduced in every way
I walked out into the sun
Amidst the trees, other people, under a blue sky
Found myself at Mariposa gluten free bakery in
the Ferry Building
Where a little voice prompted me
to buy a lemon vanilla poundcake (*also dairy
free of course*)
First thing in twenty years to remind of my
Grandma's angel food cake
One bite and the universe went all perfect
Yeah, I continue to wrestle with a demon
who's had my number since day one
I lose and I lose and I lose
Then with a mouth full of Heaven
I say, *Oh—*
Hi Grandma
You're in my heart, too!
Take a hike devil
You're out of your depths

Mary Gayle Thomas

Born and raised in Texas, Mary Gayle (MG) Thomas now lives in San Francisco. Her working career was mostly spent editing other people's writing. Now retired, she leads memoir-writing classes for the Community Living Campaign and at the Glen Canyon Rec Center. MG's work has been published on the SF Library's *Poem of the Day* website, in *Sparkle & Blink*, and the e-zine *Persimmon Tree*. She also read her poems at RAWdance's 2022 event "Step/Song/Story."

The Force

The term "force of nature" should be restricted for use exclusively in reference to my eldest brother, Brad. He can look at a situation and see solutions where no one else saw a problem.

In 1977, the hearts and minds of hundreds of thousands of people in the U.S. were blown away by the movie *Star Wars*. I'm absolutely sure no one else saw the problem with *Star Wars* that Brad saw.

The last time he watched the movie was at a drive-in theater. He sat in his car, with his camera and multiple rolls of film, taking photos of the credits. Every name, every line, every credit—from the actors to the caterers—was captured on film, which he had developed into slides. Brad then called together a group of family and friends at his house in Berkeley for a working party (emphasis on party). As people gathered, the weed got rolled and the sake got poured. Most of us had no idea what Brad was thinking. After he explained it, even fewer of us knew what he was thinking.

Brad gave an impassioned speech about world politics and détente and creativity in the free world, about the cold war and the shocking, unimaginable reality that the Russian people might never see *Star Wars*! Well, by God, this ragtag group of half-baked Berkeley stoners would take care of that.

Our mission that night, between hits of weed and sips of sake, was to watch those slides and write down the name of every person involved with the making of *Star Wars*. The goal was to contact them all. (Remember, it's 1977. We didn't have the internet. We had phone books.) Somehow, we would do the research and find out how to contact these people. Then Brad, with his Svengalian skills of persuasion, would convince those people to … Do Something.

Tony rolled the joints and Sally kept the beer flowing. Greg and Larry settled on squeaky folding chairs with clipboards and several sheets of notebook paper, while I sat cross-legged on the floor. We all had pens and paper, ready to receive our instructions.

Brad manned the slide projector. He displayed the first (of oh, so many) slides, and the project began. If a slide had four credits on it, Brad would point to individuals in turn, "You write down the first, you write the second, you take the third," so the data gathering would go more quickly. Even so, it was a long evening, made longer by the drink and smoke, but eventually, the job was done. All the names were written down and handed over to Brad, who would take the next steps. Tired and high, we went home.

About a week later, after not hearing any updates, I went to my other brother (because I didn't want to wind Brad up) and asked him what was happening with the *Star Wars* project. Herb hadn't heard anything new, and neither had anyone else. Brad had already tired of that effort. His new vision? Importing geckos from South America.

The Crazy Part

To be clear, I was not trying to commit suicide. I just wanted out the damn car. My then-husband, David, was driving. I was in the passenger seat listening to him yell during his argument-du-jour. When yelling didn't get what he deemed an appropriate response, he started punching me in the side of my head to punctuate his points. He was driving in the slow lane of I-80 somewhere around Pinole, and I thought, This is crazy. I'll just open the door, jump, and roll out onto the shoulder. There's no traffic so I won't be hit by a car. I'll get away, at least for a while. Sure, it'll probably hurt but so what? I'm already being hurt.

I opened the passenger car door and—physics happened. Opening a car door at 60 mph is virtually impossible. I didn't have so much as one foot outside the car when David grabbed my neck and pulled me toward him. My door slammed shut by itself, and he drove me straight to the County Mental Hospital.

During the intake session, I calmly explained several times that I wasn't trying to kill myself, I just wanted out the damn car. The intake clerk calmly explained several times, in so many words, that "that be crazy."

Then she said I would spend the next three days with them explaining how I didn't want to kill myself. My eyes grew wide and my heart lifted. Really? For 72 hours, I'll get three hots and a cot *and* no David?! Where do I sign up?

This episode happened in 1984, a full decade before the Violence Against Women Act was enacted. What happened wasn't illegal. If he had hit some guy in a bar, that would have been battery. Hitting his wife, however, was a private family matter.

I had a few individual sessions in the mental hospital. One pleasant meeting was held outside, where I talked to the therapist while I swung back and forth on a swing. I was also in group sessions. One day in group, I mentioned how mad I was at my brother. The counselor stood me up, brought me to the middle of the circle with him, and said, "Pretend I'm him…" He turned away to explain to the group what we were going to do, but I had already physically pounced and started beating my fists on his back. Turned out they thought that be crazy, too. That earned me another day there.

Otherwise, it was absolutely lovely. I didn't have to go to work. I didn't have to cook. I went to bed when I wanted and I slept easily.

Too soon, my time there ended and David picked me up. I sat in that same passenger seat reviewing the past few days. Was the crazy part where I tried to open a car door to get away? Or the part where they handed me back over to my abuser? Now that be crazy.

Return

I'm on a beach somewhere in Mexico with my parents. Five years old, wearing a simple blue one-piece swimsuit. I sit on the wet sand looking out toward the ocean, an inconceivably large body of water. The waves come toward me but don't touch me, and then recede, only to repeat this time and time again.

Had I ever seen a wave before? Surely not. When I was growing up in the Texas desert, the closest thing to a wave I ever saw was in a bathtub. But here I was, covered in suntan lotion, the sand and I both warmed by the sun, and looking at an endless expanse of water. Again and again, the waves encroach, closer and closer. I cry out, "Oh no!" when one recedes. When it returns, I say, "Here it comes," and when it finally sloshes over my outstretched legs I shriek as only a five-year-old can, in utter joy. I laugh and laugh.

Fifty years later the ocean spoke to me:

I see you, girl. You've come back to me again.
When I saw you that first time,

When my waves licked at your feet,
I knew I had you.
You will always come back to me.
We don't need words.
You stare and drink me up
without touching me, enraptured.
My waves don't bore you like they do others.
Calmly you gaze at the horizon,
then back to the shore
where I can tickle your feet again.
Each wave is different,
every splash is new to your eyes.

But my sounds are the same,
the same,
the same,
sweet predictability.

Roger Underhill

For Roger E. Underhill, creativity once seemed only in books. Tried copying comics/cartoons and did a short art-school stint, got an economics B.A. Dreamed undersea-scapes. Did Navy officer school, undersea photography, a bit of film school, and screenplays. Engaged in singles-club fun, sail club too, then a big S.F. volleyball mixed league. So got paid to play, coach, and referee. Writing down dreams, memorable adventures, and political hits.

Rock, Stones, and Gems of Our Lives

The Rolling Stones and the magazine and all the other musicians who, yeah, the Who too, were gems that gave us sparkle and shine.

Great wavelengths of added color.

Some of the liveliest enthralling music we could imagine.

The chance to share, and coordinate dancing to the rhythms, with current and new friends, adding excitement to our lives, and sometimes heartbreak.

Then other tunes consoled, serenaded, or rocked us back to our energetic lives. Ready to go again.

The fragrance of perfume and cologne's bite were part of the magic, usually overcoming any sweat and tears.

More satisfying than a ring with garnet, onyx, topaz, amethyst, or tourmaline, since emeralds (my birthstone), rubies, sapphires, and diamonds were overly expensive. Who knew which were real anyway?

And when I finally did get a gold ring with a deep red, glowing offset ruby in Thailand, it was later stolen.

My gold college class ring imitates emerald just fine with its deep shine and two Greek fraternity letters engraved on the top facet.

Best to just stick with the music—that's real.

So much and such variety, not only rock and roll and swing, but blues, country, soul, throbbing electronic, and finally some of the coolest rap.

And no more sting of acrid dance-club cigarette smoke, at least in the USA.

Life's gem-sparkled highlights.

Is That You, Mr. Martin?

How about the wonderful Corporatocracy? A formula for progress and compassion, right? The corporation as person, with a giant building for all the people within, is now the equivalent of a living human. Can anyone walk up to and talk to a Chevron or Lockheed Martin? Is that you, Mr. Martin? And how many lawyers can you hire, compared with the average real person fighting corporate pollution?

After World War II there was actually the building of a middle class and a social consciousness. Antitrust laws gave people more independence. That was to the chagrin of bankers and billionaires, who began plotting to regain and control assets and the media narrative: Associate socialism with communist dictators' oppression to make it—along with social security—a bad word. Then bash other the social programs for which government is designed. Commune and comrade—the base word for camaraderie—become dirty words. Next, target taxpayer funds for schools, roads, libraries, to name a few, and start to privatize. Create corporate protection in place of consumer protection. (Thanks to Ralph Nader for the latter.)

Money as free speech has captured and captivated the Republican Party's collusion with corporations for power and for the acquisition of even more money, with help from a few Democrats, like Senator Joe Manchin. (Benito Mussolini defined fascism as government in hand with corporations, although corporations were to be charted based on benefits to society.)

In the 1980s came control of newspapers and airwaves, and gutting of U.S. antitrust regulations. So—use propaganda like Nazi Germany to break down democracy with misinformation and distracting entertainment to further the country's divide and widen the inequality gap. And push the impulse to buy, buy, buy all the time, as if it were the ultimate, sexy gratification.

Venture—or rather vulture—capitalists claim that private businesses are more efficient than government programs. That theory is disproved when they take over small businesses, cut services and staff to the bone, send the companies into bankruptcy, and run off rich with the assets—as did Senator Mitt Romney with Bain Capital.

They call this free-for-all a free market. Bankers need to clean up somewhere, besides providing poor countries easy credit, then profiteering from failing economies and avoiding blame as people flee poverty and oppression. Corporate design deems its profits for owners and shareholders progress. All else is secondary and subverted to this goal. Without effective regulations, the system is just a robot crashing through the forest of society. The 2010 Supreme Court ruling on Citizens United sounded like a deal for citizens—yes, for corporate citizens with massive money that became the equivalent of free speech. Imagine yourself, as an individual, competing to buy up airtime to have your voice heard.

How often have you talked to your elected officials about what you want or think we need? Is there really free speech? Do we have a middle class anymore?

Notice that socialism for rich corporations is called a subsidy, as if it were an economic boost, but investing in people's real needs is termed undeserved welfare. In fact, investing in public welfare is good for all of us. The superrich believe they're the chosen ones to rule all others, and nature besides. Declaring spending on public welfare much too expensive, they see the expansion of military spending as a no-problem debt, as it pads their riches and power.

We have a Constitutional Corporatocracy.

§

Downtown Oakland Senior Center

Kittye Winn

Adrionne Beasley, writing as Kittye Winn, is a retired attorney and United Methodist ordained minister who now has the time to pursue her passion for writing and exploring the many faces of poetry. Since retirement, Kittye has enjoyed sharing a Friday poetry workshop with a group of talented poets, exploring the craft of poetry and story writing with Litquake writers, and a Wednesday morning group of memoir writers from the Downtown Oakland Senior Center.

Running Away

Hunkering down in a stony corner waiting for a crack in the darkness, listening for a howl, a scream, a whisper that pulverizes silence; wishing for that one dream of walking in cotton candy, picking caramel corn from stalks and chocolate dew dripping on her protruding tongue; mama humming precious lord take my hand, daddy wrapped around her like ivy vines. So she waits and hunkers and shivers and listens and stares at the dark and wishes. Until at first light the geese fly over in V formation honking and shitting white goo onto her threadbare shoes.

Bless the Mess

(from off the cuff poems)

God bless this mess I have made of
this junk stacked to 5 feet and three
this garbage of a mind

God bless that You too often sit at my edge
when I need You at my middle
doubled over in pain

God bless my stretched-out feelings
my temperament untwined
can't help not caring—can't find the time

God bless my voice screaming
until my throaty rasp is all I can muster
when my truth is asked for—lies I mime

God bless the bomb beneath me counting down
until the end—I can't defuse the wired confusion
to save myself from the boom

God bless my cries, eyes streaming

onto my swollen leaking breast.
God please kiss-heavy
my hands
my heart
my feet.

To Become a Poet

after Nikki Giovanni

To become a poet it is important to
set your body, your heart, your mind
free.
Breathe into your soul the truth
but only the truly hashed-out truth
no stretched-out, hidden-note lies
no covered-up tunes, no lost or dropped beats
gotta
pay attention to spot the zings that
ping and pong through the air bouncing
over the world, reaching out into the
universe
searching for the absolutes that set truth
free
to bless you while frisking you
down into your deepest pockets where
dust mites are gathering around
shards of old peppermint candy gunk
grandma used to shut you up on Sundays
while the preacher's preaching
gotta

pay attention to fill in the stillness
splashing lights and shadows shuffling
over the rooms where you
sleep and eat and write
opening
your eyes that stare unblinking
into the abyss waiting and hoping that
when the truth reveals itself without blemish
your *Ah Ha!* moment
will spread itself
across your page.

Hell's Cool Midst

after Katie Farris

In the midst of hell—a place
Within the flames a cool center—calling
your mind to seek—calling
your body to leap beyond the fear—calling
you to deny impossibility
and beckon all probability that
somewhere love with all Her power
is ever there where you need Her to be.

You cringe at the thought of
your inability to comprehend
your shoulders hunch in disbelief
you yell *stop the bus let me off*
you ring the bell to end
this horrific ride—run, hide

But in this burning hole—moving
quickly toward the abyss
you scrunch, shielding from its slow burn
even the drenching with life's hoses
bring no relief—you wish

for that place in hell's cool midst where
in a slop of shadows you'll kneel—you pray
stirring up a new stew of faith.

You want to believe
you want to trust
through hope's elusive flickering—you search
dare to rise, dare to step—then you leap
toward the promised—you grasp, you grip
then maybe soon—you'll find You
in a holy place even in the midst of hell.

Tanna Bellia

Tanna Bellia, who resides in Oakland, is both a painter and a poet. She says: "The day I joined a poetry class was the day I was reborn."

She Plays All Day

Curly hair, feathers of a raven
Lover of keys wedded to a piano
She comforts herself each day
Banging the pedals with both feet
Quivering fingers at play
She plays all day
Energy moving thru her body
Tilting tone upside down
She plays all day
She plays all day
Melodies morning into night
Her aliveness, a blaze from within

Hot tones bleating beats dipped in bravery
Rapture of sound from the desert floor
A keyboard shaped by ardor
A tornado plotting explosion
Moving like the sting of a bee
Awakening fire from dead coals
Speeding vehicle needing no battery
Buried chords from a wild heart
The damper sits on the tip of keys

Tingling tipsy from laughter and longing
Bathing her children in waves of song
Mother is the boogie woogie flow of love

Where Do I Dwell if not in Possibility?

A language I read thru a closed door
twisting my soft spot
an oracle of whimsy, rectory of light
blowing hard thru blind words
listen to the sound of mother playing the piano
comforts herself with a scrunch of
    Scaramouche
sung by a tenor with no name

Where do I dwell if not in possibility
damp brisk of a carved happiness
roaming thru my filtering heart
angels playing with the flow of love
heading home again from every nook
and cranny of God's creation
no filters found here only truth

The slop of shadow disappearing
in the panoply of ecstasy
sliding slowly into a warm dust of sound
mother loves to play the piano
the act ends at ten, we watch

they rise to stoke the doorway of meaning
a coaxial cable waiting for touch to heal me
render me whole and complete again
like Venus moving into Gemini

I Am

after Edith Södergran

I am a woman, a female, a she
I am a lover, a lusty kiss from the altar of awareness
I am a whisper of existence in a red velvet blessing
I am a leap into freedom and the self

I am an electric dream of sacred desire
I am an exotic flame with a bold impulse to soar
I am a mother to 100,000 singing roses
I am a portal of chance and possibility

I am the golden doors of aliveness
When I don't know, I simply make it up as I go

She Was

a tender kiss freely offered to all,
a jockey on a philly who can't gallop.

A philly who can no longer gallop
is an earthsong held in porcelain.

An earthsong held in porcelain between
my trembling fingertips permeates

my trembling fingertips, permeates
the room, seizes the throat with craving,

craving desire, beneficent grace.
Her words gave place, cut through time & space.

Her words gave place in a moment of impact.
The whole world waits swimming in the clouds—

The whole world waits outside the doggy door,
a tender kiss freely offered to all.

Zakiyyah G.E. Capehart

Zakiyyah G.E. Capehart-Bolling is a writer, published poet, storyteller, performance artist, visual artist, and radio producer/host. Her artistic skills combined with a medical background allow her to produce shows that help educate and heal communities. Her poetry is published in numerous anthologies and has been shared internationally. Zakiyyah's sojourn to Ghana, West Africa, inspired her first book of poems and short stories, *Ghana on My Mind*.

A Tragic Accident

Jessica was asleep when Clinton got home. He woke her when he slammed the front door. The spring from the door hinge, already loose, fell off when he closed the door. Jessica heard it roll across the floor. Abruptly, Clinton stumbled across the living room. She glanced at the clock on the nightstand. It was 3 a.m., and he was drunk again. He tripped and fell as he approached their bedroom. She heard him scurry to his feet.

The bedroom door opened and the ceiling light flooded the room. Clinton began speaking to Jessica incoherently, the foul odor from his breath like rotten garbage. Jessica asked Clinton to cut off the light because it was piercing her eyes. He advanced toward her, eyes blazing and the fire of vile words spitting from his mouth. This was nothing new; Jessica was familiar with this behavior. She decided she didn't want to tolerate it anymore. Clinton punched Jessica in the face, and her eyes watered and throbbed. She could feel her lips swelling from the force of his huge hands.

Jessica ran from the bedroom into the kitchen. Clinton followed. Trembling and sobbing, she pleaded with him to stop, as she reached for the butcher's knife. In a rage he advanced toward her. Jessica held the knife in her hands, hoping to stop him. But he moved closer, stumbled, tripped, and fell on Jessica. Jessica said she heard Clinton's desperate needy moan when the knife entered his chest.

Jessica sits on her cot in the prison cell she occupies, reminiscing about her life before that fatal night. She frequently ponders: if Clinton were alive she would be free.

Mark F. DeWitt

Mark F. DeWitt is a retired professor of music, long-time Zen student, and short-time poet. He lives in Oakland, and is author of the book *Cajun and Zydeco Music in Northern California: Modern Pleasures in a Postmodern World.*

What Is a Cross?

after Susan Elizabeth Howe

What is all the fuss about, a
couple of lines that cross a bit
above the middle, at a right angle?

a swastika minus the outer lines,
but then the lines acquire a third
dimension and that's where the trouble begins,

with a story. Lines become beams and beams
become lashed together to support
the lashed, the last person you would ever

think would become an everlasting
hero. Believers can tell you the rest.
I call that number, I get no answer.

Vertical plus horizontal equals hysterical,
burning in the front yard, so he
went down to the crossroads, got down on his

knees, got nailed in the crosswalk, listened
to the crosstalk and got no answers, except
vertical plus horizontal equals homicidal.

The old rugged cross went onward,
marching off to war, going on as before.
A wit once said to never trust

a man with two first names. It stands
therefore to reason not to trust
a sign with two straight lines.

I'll not die on that hill, but the
story never dies. In the shadow
of the cross, I will rest, says the hymn,
but not me, not now, not ever.

D. Fromm

D. Fromm lives in Berkeley.

Cars Poetica

This rock just sits there.
Words though are juicy and can splat

driving eyes from here to there in
nothing flat.

Why this sleeping and snoring?
Poke it. Punch down the gas.

Swerve, cuuurve, rock, crack!
Poems turn this into that.

Engraved

I woke up in the middle of the night and stared at my alarm clock, which was covered with a book that I moved aside very quietly. I could see the red dial: 2:35. I turned over.

Then went to pee, then got back into bed, then slowly in darkness counted my breaths. Semi-waking, semi-sleeping, I was visited by mom who said that her grave didn't look finished—wasn't tidy like the others. I told her we were deciding about her marker. had been emailing about it.

I was thinking a gray stone marker, which looked solid. She shook her head. She didn't like it.

"Lori mentioned bronze," I said, "and that looks good."

"No," she said, "not bronze."

"No?"

"It will look dirty after a little while."

"OK," I said, "they also have beautiful black ones."

"Not black. I don't like so much black. So dark."

"Well, there's white..."

"White like my kitchen. It looks clean."

She liked the white. Then asked what takes so long. I said there was a difference of opinion. I said we were searching for the words. We would speed it up. I thought of how I missed her. How there was no one to wrap me in a caring embrace.

I wondered again: how do you love someone who is critical? Mom seemed to be someone who could care for those who weren't particularly accepting of her.

"How do you do that?" I asked.

She had understood, in her day, how to stay at home, dress up, red lipstick, be the polite and kind wife; the kind of role I couldn't abide nor could she understand. Though love was her guide, and mine was old flannel shirts and Levi's with holes that she hid or tossed aside.

"Wouldn't it be better," she remarked, "if you wore these tights?" Suggestions flowed: redo your hair, your nails, your eyes.

Anger doesn't suit you. Be nice.

She favored pinks and white; I didn't want to match with sacrifice. It took years to understand those dual dueling strands: that deep feeling of love and her wish that I were different, "better" than what I am.

Wanting more of what is not there. Mom-reflector that I am, I wrote this and handed it to her. She, who in my dream was both small and bigger than the two of me, inscribed her arms around us.

I went back to lie down.

Though we had many opinions on her grave marker, we ordered a white one engraved with a red rose.

She hasn't said a word.

Julie R. Hawthorne

Julie Hawthorne, a writer living in Oakland, grew up in Hanover, New Hampshire, and enjoys both coasts. A retired clinical social worker, she is happy to have the opportunity now to pursue her latent passion. First inspired to write when her mother wrote a genealogy and a children's story, Julie is working on short stories. She's looking forward to experimenting with magical realism.

Notes from Memorial Day 2023

Even though World War II didn't affect me directly—none of my close relatives fought overseas—the generation of my peers was plagued by fathers with PTSD. And by mothers' secret distress.

My mom had a first marriage. When I discovered this, at about 12, she brushed it off. "He went crazy during the beginning of the war," she said. The subject was closed.

As the war had progressed, my mom worked as a weather-map plotter at MIT, during the time when chaos theory was being developed. She was support staff, a college friend of the chief chaos scientist's wife. She fell in love with one of the engineers, but the man returned to his marriage. She was devastated. Years later, coming out of a semi-coma, she talked in her sleep about Boston. She wanted to return to the place where she'd been truly, inescapably, in love.

The war ended. Everyone was getting married. The pressure was on: my mom wanted a family. She feared growing too old. She settled for a guy she felt was attractive. They would make beautiful babies together; she was a looker herself.

The emotional results were disastrous. Though she denies they were ever happy, I saw a photo of their one-year anniversary: both were smiling. And I was born.

Perhaps I should thank World War II for my existence. Perhaps I should thank the after-war marriage boom. Yet, of course, I don't. I mourn the casualties. I struggle to understand.

Irene Kane

Irene Kane was born and raised in Pittsburgh, Pennsylvania. She has participated in classes with Litquake through the Downtown Oakland Senior Center, authoring life stories to share with family back East. She writes and performs ceremonies for weddings and end-of-life celebrations in the greater Bay Area as owner of *www.ceremoniesandcelebrations.com*.

Tired Peonies (Memory and Gratitude)

Looking at a tired bouquet of peonies on my table, I wondered, toss them all or find at least one to salvage? The once rose-tinted blooms standing so upright were now white with brown edges and drooping forward—begging to be released into the compost.

As I considered the fate of these blossoms, I was reminded of Yoshie Akiba arranging flowers at the entrance to her restaurant and jazz club, Yoshi's.

I had stopped at the Jack London box office one afternoon to pick up show tickets and noticed Yoshie creating a welcoming floral arrangement on the restaurant side of the business. Calm and focused, she took her time positioning, removing, stepping back, appraising. Not satisfied, she brought out a Buddha statue, and said quietly, "Maybe this will help me," as she incorporated Buddha into her display.

I had read that Yoshie grew up in an orphanage in Japan. She once commented in an interview that music and dance helped her express the pain and sorrow she experienced when her parents died. She later left Japan, moving to Baltimore, then on to Berkeley to study dance. During her years in Berkeley, she and a few business partners opened Yoshi's Japanese Restaurant, taking it through several iterations and locations to the current Yoshi's Oakland.

During the pandemic closures, my partner, Frank, and I missed attending jazz events there. When the club reopened, we were excited to return for a taste of something almost normal. We arrived with proofs of vaccination and N95 masks, eager to see and hear Poncho Sanchez leading his Latin Jazz Band. On the way into the club, I noticed Yoshie quietly enjoying her meal at the restaurant side. The club filled up, we found our seats, ordered drinks, and settled in to the pulsating Latin rhythms. During a slower number I noticed someone slinking along in a colorful flowing dress, arms overhead, smiling like the Buddha, totally in her element. Another side of Yoshie Akiba emerged as she danced her way to stage left. Her gentle, easeful movements never overshadowed the musicians; she was an additional instrument. I was awed by her bravery and inhibition. I wanted to join her.

The orphaned young girl had found comfort from her grief in graceful dancing. That evening I found comfort, I let go of a little sadness from those pandemic years when hundreds of thousands died, lives were turned upside down, and life as we knew it was permanently altered.

As I emptied the peony petals into the compost, I kept one slightly faded bloom to remind me of Yoshie Akiba's spontaneity and elegance, and the power of music and dance to soothe the soul.

Journeys

I don't remember how I found the imaginary playmate I named Journey. Some family members thought it was Granny's parting words, "Safe journey," as various relatives and visitors said their goodbyes when leaving our house.

We lived in my mom's childhood home with Granny and Mom's oldest sister, Aunt Mary—an arrangement my parents intended as temporary when they began married life toward the end of wartime, in 1943. I had lots of adult attention and oversight, sometimes too much. I was three or four; none of my siblings had arrived yet. I imagine I created Journey to have a companion, someone to sit on the steps with, plan adventures, slurp cherry popsicles on the green awning-covered front porch, or pick pink hollyhocks in the empty lot next door.

When I attended Oakland's Neighbors Night Out several years ago, helping participants to sign in and get a name tag, it had been a long time since I remembered those days at Granny's.

A friendly dad named Ben arrived carrying his daughter snuggled in a Baby Björn carrier.

"How about a name tag for your baby?" I asked. When he wrote down her name, I was speechless for a moment. I asked, "Her name is Journey?" "Yes," Ben answered. "Her mom picked it out." It felt magical, like a part of my childhood was validated. What if I had changed my name to Journey, a name of my own choosing? Who would I be now? I felt I was destined to meet this beautiful child, "almost" a namesake.

During the pandemic, as neighbors took walks to break free from isolation, Journey came by to check up on my flowers, and I taught her my grandma name, Nini, by illustrating one knee, two knees, *Ni ni*. When Journey turned five recently, I asked her dad if they could stop by. "I used to be in TK, but now I graduated into kindergarten at Anna Yates School," she told me.

She has a sturdy erect posture, chestnut brown skin, and a smiling face framed with tousled black curls. She wore a floppy fuchsia hat, seemed comfortable in herself and very skilled handling her shih tzu poodles, Chip

Dip and Sofie Lee. She made sure to explain that the poodles shared the family's last name. I learned she had Thanksgiving breakfast and Thanksgiving lunch—do you know where I had lunch? she asked. "No," I replied. "At my uncle's firehouse and I got to sit on a fire truck and hold, you know," she said, gesturing the movements of a steering wheel. "And then I had Thanksgiving dinner."

Will our paths continue to cross on our life journeys? Will Journey continue to be the goodwill ambassador she is now? Our futures are unknown, but I'm grateful to this very alive Journey friend.

Irene Sardanis

Irene is a retired psychologist and published author out of the Bronx, New York, who now calls the Bay home.

Kathy, the Bead Lady

We met in a Friday morning writing class at the library. Kathy never told me her age, and I kept a low profile about mine, but I knew we were the only two senior ladies in the group. She was known as Kathy, the Bead Lady, and after class one day, she invited me to have coffee at her art studio in Emeryville.

Around the room were tables of bins of beads in blues, greens, reds, oranges.

When I put my hands in the beads, they spoke to me. They made sounds like, “Oh, yes, do that some more; move me around, hold me in your hand.”

Kathy loved the sound of her clients moving around her studio with their hands in the bead bins—people making selections for a necklace or bracelet. They may just have been beads, but these baubles were like sparkling gems.

Although I was never one for jewelry—hardly ever wore earrings or a necklace—still, didn’t I already have a drawer full of boxes of Cartier and other accessories from Tiffany’s that my wealthy sister had sent me from New York? Heavens, what would I do with one more necklace?

Kathy and I always met at her studio. She'd fix a cup of tea for us and we'd sit around her table and talk. Her place was like a small art museum. I loved being surrounded by the sparkling beads, the gems, her large abstract paintings and sculptures. She always dressed stylishly, with bright colored blouses; her face all made up, like she had a hot date. Kathy would look at me and say, "We have to doll you up, honey." She'd fix my collar. "You have to put some color on you, some burgundies and violets." Kathy would go into her closet and bring out colorful scarves to drape around my neck. "Try these on," she'd say, patting my face affectionately. "And stop wearing black."

I missed the signs that she wasn't doing well. She'd cancel some of our meetings to see doctors and take tests. Too late, she was diagnosed with Stage 4 leukemia. When she started chemo and radiation treatments, she canceled our coffee dates. Kathy lost all her gorgeous, thick red hair. Her vibrant scarves could hide her bald head but did not cover her depression. Eventually, Kathy stopped seeing me and other friends.

Kathy is gone now, yet I still remember her art studio, the squishing of the beads in the bins—my fingers touching and playing with the marblelike globules, the sound of their click-click-click.

I regret never asking Kathy to make something creative for me, a necklace to just toss over my head, so I could touch the beads as though they were religious objects, and remember how loved I felt when Kathy and I were together.

Trickster

The trickster in my life was my mother–the master manipulator. If she walked into the room, you'd see a poor, pudgy immigrant looking sad, bent over wearing a soiled housecoat, and you'd feel sorry for her. You'd want to offer a chair for her, offer her a glass of tea to show pity for her condition.

My mother managed to have four children do all her bidding—to translate for her, go to medical appointments, run errands—and be her interloper for anything she didn't want to deal with. I was the caregiver who rubbed her arms and served her tea in bed, listened to her laments, and encouraged her to leave her depressed bed. Nothing worked.

I wanted to please this trickster in my life, to dance to her tune—but the price was too high. Nothing given was enough. No amount of service to her needs was sufficient. Yet, I felt tricked by believing if only I did what she wanted—even go to church and pray to God to give her good health, well then, she'd be thankful to me, her obedient servant. She would appreciate and love me for my goodwill to cure her of all her ailments.

Trickster. I truly believed if I obeyed my mother and followed her suffering footsteps, I'd get rewarded and appreciated. But that was never to be. That trickster mother of mine had endless needs and wishes that no one could satisfy. With all my good deeds to please her, I hoped that maybe I could trick her back. My mother would stand back and see all the things I did to serve her and she'd be grateful, open her arms with love and embrace me. What a joke.

The trickster always wins in the end, grinding the believer into the ground, defeated. Unless, of course, the one being tricked stops playing the game and walks away.

Greek Easter

What I remember most about Greek Easter was the imposed fasting. Everyone in the family was instructed to eat nothing with meat, fish, oil, and dairy. We were poor so I was always hungry for food like hamburgers, mac and cheese and especially pizza. During the time of lent I was always looking for anything I could eat.

As a child my Greek immigrant mother would prepare the family for Greek Easter by fasting for 40 days. She wanted to follow Jesus, who fasted for 40 days before he was crucified.

What foods could this hungry teenager eat during this fasting period? Bread, tea, and one of those awful bland-tasting lentil soup called *Faki* that my mother made. While this interminable fast went on, I'd go back and forth into the kitchen looking for something to eat. I'd look into the ice box, but it was empty with only stale inedible left-over food we should have thrown out.

I am ashamed to admit that as a teen, in defiance of this forced fasting, I'd go into my mother's purse and steal money. I was angry and rebellious at being required to fast. I was already hungry. Now I was starving. I'd grab the pilfered money to meet with friends and share a pizza together.

I'd meet my friends at the local soda shop at the corner, and we'd go four blocks away to Gino's for pizza. After we ordered one with pepperoni, I salivated with the aromas coming from the kitchen oven. I could hardly wait until it was served. When it arrived with all the melted cheese and pepperoni on it, I'd gobble my piece and look for more. Oh, it felt so good to eat something real and tasty. Later, I felt a stomachache.

Afterwards I was no longer hungry, but I'd feel guilty for having taken money from my poor mother's purse. I could not face her. Although I was a disobedient teenager, I still felt remorse.

Everyone in the family was expected to go to church for all the services during the week prior to Easter. Saturday night was the longest where the church service went on and on until about one a.m. We'd have to stand for most of it.

One late Easter Eve service at midnight, I was tired and got up to leave. My mother pointed to my seat and ordered, "Where do you think you're going? Sit down. The service is not over. You can't leave."

Sunday, Greek Easter was the day of the big feast. All the relatives came over, the aunts and cousins from Astoria, dressed up and ready to celebrate. "*Christos Anesti*," they said. Christ has risen.

My mother would make roast lamb with garlic and oregano in the oven for the main course. The house was fragrant with the aromas of garlic, oregano, and roasted lamb, the table full of salads, cheese and olives.

Fast forward to the present. I still celebrate Greek Easter except I do not go to church or fast anymore. The Easter food celebration is now at a park with California friends, not my New York family.

It's good to be Greek and celebrate Easter, but I'm glad that I'm not back in New York, attending the long church services and fasting for forty days. Those days for me are over.

The Past

Forgetting is hard
Forgiving is harder
Listening to Greek music, I dance
Loving I need to practice
I let go

I let go
Listening to Greek music, I dance
Forgiving is hard
Forgetting is harder
Loving—I need to practice

Paula J. Shadle

Paula Shadle is a retired scientist living in Oakland. A published technical writer, she now writes poetry and is at work on a family memoir based on grandparents' tales and various records.

The Street Booth

Nettie and Wanda sold cigars and chocolate at their small street booth in downtown Chicago. The sisters practiced their English with passersby; in between, they had lively conversations in German to while away the time. Most of the passersby were also recent immigrants, from Eastern Europe or Germany. The collapse of the Polish-Lithuanian empire had driven them to seek a future in America. The city was crammed with younger sons who would never inherit, and daughters who had been brought along as cheap labor and the hope of marrying into a more prosperous life. Meanwhile, everyone waited and worked very hard.

Nettie had no such prospects. She had a hunched back and uneven gait; a childhood accident had broken her back and it healed crooked. She amused herself by making up names and stories for the more colorful bachelors who passed by. Turkey-Legs was a young man with legs so skinny that he did look birdlike. Red-Cabbage Man had russet hair, slicked down with oil, and a sour expression reminiscent of a startled ferret.

Nettie was the first to notice that Herr Priess was coming regularly to buy cigars. He was a sausage maker and butcher, or *Metzger*, and had recently arrived, in 1907. He had a large smile and booming laugh, and the sisters agreed that his English was perfectly awful.

"I think Herr Hot Dog likes you, Wanda," Nettie said one day, after Herr Priess left the stand. He had stayed a while to chat with Wanda.

"Well, he is a nice gentleman," Wanda mused. "But he has a dreadful smoking habit. Look how he buys a cigar nearly every day! And he is such a greenhorn. So inexperienced in city ways and American ways… yet very handsome and quite tall. And he is two years younger than I am."

"Well, Wanda, he doesn't know that!" said Nettie.

Sure enough, Herr Hot Dog was there the very next day. He smiled at Wanda and waited patiently for her to serve him, not noticing that Nettie was ready and waiting. With a playful glint in her bright blue eyes, Nettie ventured,

"My goodness, you do buy a lot of cigars, Herr Priess!" Herr Hot Dog paused, reddened slightly, then explained that the cigars were for a friend.

Suddenly, Wanda was smiling up at him and chatting attentively. Soon she had enticed his life story out of him (the 10th child, not going to inherit, from the Rheinland). Her pale blue eyes danced as they gazed into his. He began to tell jokes, and his face lit up like a candle. He stayed at the stand a long time, and it became apparent that he would be back the next day, and perhaps not even bother to buy a cigar.

After he left, Wanda turned to Nettie. "Please stop calling him 'Herr Hot Dog,' Nettie," she warned. "His name is Wilhelm."

Nettie just laughed. She knew her sister well. Even three years' separation, while Wanda was in Chicago and before Nettie had immigrated, had not changed their rapport.

Newspaper notice, 1910:

William A. Pries and Wanda Speichert of Chicago were married on Saturday, June 3, 1910.

The bride was attended by her sisters. The groom, 24, wore a morning suit, while the bride, 22, wore a lovely white dress…

The couple will make their home in Chicago.

Coming to America

She slices open the letter with the foreign stamps and the familiar handwriting. The postmark: Chicago, Illinois, America. The envelope is addressed:

Fräulein Philippina Priess
Bosenheim, Bad Kreuznach
Germany (Deutschland)

Inside is a letter on onionskin paper and a ticket for the ship Europa, sailing from Bremen to Baltimore, Maryland, USA, on June 2, 1920. Out falls a money order for $200 U.S. currency. Her heart pounding, she unfolds the letter.

Dearest Sister Binchen,

You must see this country to believe it! If one is willing to work hard, there is money to be made and property to buy. Illinois looks a lot like Germany, with wheat and rye and corn, except the farms are enormous. My grocery store does very well. I make my own sausages and run the meat counter.

I know you will love it here. I enclose a ship ticket and money for the train to Bremen and your other expenses. I can meet you when the ship docks in Baltimore.

Loving greetings from your brother,
Wilhelm Priess (William Pries, Senior)

She drops a few tears at the familiar handwriting and holds the letter close to her heart for a moment. To go to America and never return to this village with its gossips, its narrow-mindedness, and its shortage of young men, especially any with hope in their eyes after the Great War. To think that her brother owns his own grocery store in America.

"Oh, and what should I take with me? I must take my sewing machine, so that I can make some money. And my Sunday best clothes."

"You aren't really thinking of going, are you, Binchen?" her sister asks. "Mother and Father have worked their fingers to the bone to provide for us. And you would leave them alone in their old age?"

"Why are you so mean? Wilhelm needs me too. I must take my feather beds along."

"They won't fit, Binchen," says her sister, who was not invited and besides would never leave her homeland. "You will have to leave them behind."

"Well, if I can't take my feather beds with me, I won't go!"

And I do not know even one word of English! I have never been on a ship or a train… just the tractor and the horse and carriage. I would leave my friends, my dishes, and the fields my family has tilled for 200 years. Mr. Knodel is coming for coffee and *kuchen* tomorrow. He has never said, but I do think he likes me. But maybe I can marry a farmer in Illinois.

She sits in the rocking chair in her father's house, where she was born, and thinks of Wilhelm's face when she alights from the ship. She looks around the room, saying goodbye to the lace curtains, the furniture made by her grandfather, and her mother's bag of knitting. A trip to America is a one-way voyage. Then, crying, she finds her mother in the kitchen and tells her that she will be staying.

**[Philippina (Binchen) Pries was my grandfather's younger sister. Wilhelm died in 1964, and Binchen around 1978 in Germany. After Wilhelm immigrated, they saw each other only on his one visit back home in the 1920s. Decades later, Edith, Binchen's great granddaughter, came to live with me, at age 16 or 17. She told me this story; any gaps are fictionalized.]*

Hospice

The old man in the wheelchair
Chases an elusive noun,
Once a brilliant physicist,
Knew infrared and satellites.
Ran a science club for girls
Back in the sexist sixties.

And now: Where am I?
Who pays for this?
How did my daughter get here?
Did she drive or fly?
"Dad, you are a great father."
"Back off, I'm not dying today," he grunts.

His tapered fingers hold
The cell phone gracefully.
He swivels his head and whispers
"My coffee was cut off after one cup."
Dad is proud and cowed
Taking orders from others.
"They control me," he says.

The old man naps in the armchair
Near the silent piano and the noisy TV.
His hospice home is clean and safe.
He has no one to talk to.
This one babbles nonsense;
That one talks quietly, her
Head bent into her chest.
Must lock her car yet has no car.
"Is this living?" Dad asks.
Feelings not expressed in words;
Real men suffer in silence.

The old man in the small room
Sees the family photos on the shelf.
"Will I ever go home?" he asks.
He knows the answer.
His daughter cries quietly
In the corner
While he sleeps.

The old man in the hospital bed
Dreads pain and loss.
He is letting go
One memory at a time.

I hold his hand.
This is what daughters do.

He sips and savors the soup.
Today he is alive.
Go home, daughter, and live your life.

The old man lies in bed.
He gasps for air.
Oxygen helps but little.
Still alert, he asks me again
Who is paying?
The government, we say.

Today it is raining.
Our crying is a river.
His grandson enters,
Baby girl in his arms.
The man lights up like a candle
Long kept on a shelf.
Dad's hand holds her foot
As she smiles with her five teeth.
Four generations fit in this
Tiny hospice room.

Oxygen machine purrs
As we hold his hand
And share his joy
For a shining moment.

Susan Steinhauer

Susan Steinhauer lives in Oakland. She enjoys writing about nature, food, cooking, and people.

The Gift

The delivery interrupts the gray monotony on Route 1, Hendricks, WV 26271 on a cold February day. The leafless trees surround the willow by the front pond. On this day, the dirt road to the mobile double-wide trailer is frozen enough that the brown UPS truck can drive through the gate from Route 72 and not run the risk of getting mired in mud. My fragile lifeline to the outside holds.

There have been packages before this one. An umbrella stroller, perfect for the paved sidewalks of the suburbs but unsuitable for these uneven, unpaved dirt roads; beautiful children's picture books featuring shrews and mice inhabiting cozy homelike settings; and my mother's homemade ragù, frozen, then packed in dry ice and shipped to me by her butcher. A taste to sustain me after the birth of my son in 1978. When what was needed was a friendly set of hands to hold the baby, if only for a few moments. And a voice to tell me, "You have this."

Past the trailer's threshold, the door spills into a jumble of combination living room/bedroom/kitchen annex, populated with a chest freezer, a crib, a wood stove not recommended for use in a mobile home, a Scandinavian-style rope and wood chair, and a worn green Naugahyde armchair. On a shelf next to the back window sits a green plant and a radio that receives intermittent signals from WV Public Radio. The red gingham-checked curtain parts to let in some daylight.

The three of us are shoehorned into this tin box of a home. Condensation appears on the walls in the winter and the trailer bakes in the heat in the summer.

But on this day, manna arrives on that brown box truck.

Oranges and green leaves decorate the outside of the cardboard box with its return address of Hale Groves, Vero Beach, Florida. Inside the box, eight ruby red grapefruits are wrapped in tissue paper emblazoned with the company logo.

Once the driver has left, I cut and section one of the grapefruits and insert my spoon. It is succulent and sweet and tastes of home.

Barbara Tooma

Barbara Tooma is an artist's model who has been writing continually for 23 years. She is an East Coast transplant who loves California.

The Portrait

Hot pink feathered hat
Perched on a mop of wavy hair
Big blue eyes staring
Like the saucer eyes of a Cheshire cat
A nose shaped in classical mode
Roman to the core
Lips slim but sensuous
Pink-lipsticked to match the hat
One gloved hand royal blue
Resting on her rosy cheek
Matted in chalk white
Surrounded by a metallic silver frame.
A quirky vision of an eccentric woman

In the Hospital

They prayed for me
Circles of knowing people
Others were strangers who cared about God
I asked God to take me
But he wouldn't comply
I wasn't ready yet, he said,
Didn't want me then
Doesn't want me now.

Former Self, Present Self

I am not the “exotic” dark-eyed woman
Sporting waist-length tresses
I am a sylph of myself
My hair, short, thin and fine, unruly
Now a rusted red hue.
My body adorned with wrinkled skin
The flesh does not obey its mantra:
To stay firm and supple
Age spots sprinkle my arms
Like freckles on a fair-skinned face
My innards a mess of unbalanced workings
One part failing after another.
My walk a slow zigzag,
Unsteady, cane-dependent
My muscles sore, unused
Weakness substituting for strength.
All systems are not go, but gone
I mourn my former self
Her continuous motion
In a twirl of perpetual dance
A traveling muse to far-off places
Sparkling eyes, spangled earrings

Verve for life,
Enthralled by new experiences.
I crave this lost self.
I want her back.
Return to me, o wondrous woman
In spirit if not in body.
Meld the two into one.

§

Community Living Campaign: Bethel Church

Christine Arenas

Christine Rose Beccaria Arenas (Beccy) is a proud third generation San Franciscan. She attended public school and Catholic school in SF. Beccy and her husband, Peter, have lived for 46 years in the house that her grandparents bought in 1936. They have two children and five wonderful grandchildren. She worked for SFUSD as a Para Liaison from 1985-2013 and then came to Cayuga Connectors to start a new chapter in her life.

Seasons of the City

As I am a native San Franciscan, my four seasons are distinctly San Francisco seasons.

I would say spring is a favorite because everything is blooming, and I love the warmth of the sun.

Summer is usually dreary, the worst for fog. But we drive an hour for sunny warm weather in Russian River, Calistoga, or Marin, and in less time can get to the South Bay, where we find it 10 degrees warmer.

We have beautiful fall colors in SF, and if we cross the bridge, even more autumn orange, red, and yellow.

I love the twinkling lights and decorations of Christmas. I used to ski, and would go to Lake Tahoe, and once to Vail, Colorado—beautiful but very cold. I don't think I would want a whole season of snow and freezing temps.

We are blessed by San Francisco's mild weather.

Victoria Hamilton

A native San Franciscan and schoolteacher, Victoria Hamilton loved teaching arts and crafts to young children. "Never have and never will leave this beautiful City by the Bay!"

Lady Cat

Simone is the name of my pet cat. Simone used to be Frank's cat until he passed away; now Simone is all mine.

She must be close to 100 years old—cat time! I have her records filed but I'm afraid to check her age because I don't know if I can stand the thought of losing her.

Let me tell you how precious she is. She has a sable coat, smooth and shiny when I brush her hair; golden eyes and walks around the house like she is Queen Victoria.

Did I mention that her parents were show cats?

Frank, my late husband, was enamored by Simone, who is a purebred Burmese. When we brought her home, she walked down the red carpet and won best in show!

Frank never wanted her to be a show cat. He heard about Burmese cats being docile and loving to sit on laps.

Nowadays, when I'm sitting, watching TV, or reading, she automatically jumps on my lap and purrs such a soothing purr. She is old now like me, and is on meds and a special diet—like me.

I love her so much!

I love her purring …

About the Anthology

Litquake sparks critical conversations, and inspires writers and readers of all ages to celebrate the written word with diverse year-round literary programming, interactive workshops, and a ten-day festival.

Litquake's Elder Project is a literary arts project focused on creative expression and community through writing and performances. The project brings teaching artists to the elders in a classroom accessible to them. The class and writing partnerships allow students to discuss and record past and current life experiences, resulting in personal empowerment through creativity. The goal is for seniors to find new self-confidence using the creative process, writing, and performance as a means of generating a dialogue within and outside of their own community. This is writing from residents and attendees across all of the sites we serve as of June 2023: Cayuga Connectors and Life Remembered at Bethel Church through the Community Living Campaign, Downtown Oakland Senior Center,

Dr. George Davis Senior Center in Bayview, and the San Francisco Campus for Jewish Living.

The classes meet weekly in a grid of Zoom rectangles, or at tables pushed together to make one space. Students and instructors come to class not just to write, but more significantly, to be together, to find community, to hear our voices. To outwit isolation. We come together for "plainspoken, undeniably wise undeniably loving advice...," as Greg Taylor writes in his incantatory poem "I Was Told by Forces I Do Not Understand to Come Share This Exact Thing with You."

In this anthology, you read about the kid who, on a drive through bucolic '60s Tennessee, gets a matter-of-fact lesson in racism from his dapper Uncle Roy. You meet a Jewish youth assigned a Nazi to tutor him in German in the late '40s, a story told in sly deadpan. In the '50s, a girl parked with her boyfriend on a runway is interrupted in their make-out session by the sudden shriek of a military jet. Dancing ensues.

A lot of dancing appears in this collection—as does love, for friends, partners (those alive and those gone), dogs, cats, horses, and the sight of moonlight at 5 a.m. Parents continue to confound the writers, a half-century after they left home. (As D. Fromm writes: "Semi-waking, semi-sleeping, I was visited by mom / who said that her grave didn't look finished...") You hear about war (WWII, war with Korea, the Cold War, not to mention Star Wars), and rage between spouses (in fiction and nonfiction). You'll travel to Indiana, Coney Island, Japan, and of course our beloved, imperfect Bay Area.

The landscape of loss—called by Grace D'Anca "an emotional North and South Dakota—" coexists in these pages with consolation, humor, and great happiness. Doris Beers refers to "small, spangled measures of hope." And throughout the anthology, as Naomi Cooper writes, "people take this risk / of surrendering impermeability, becoming / so gorgeous in their courage."

These writers take the long view, sending dispatches from a world whose contours aren't as well-mapped as those of youth and middle age. If you are an elder yourself, as you page back through the anthology, you feel the impulse to speak the many truths discovered over a long, rich life.

A special thank you to California Arts Council, the Joseph & Vera Long Foundation, and the Artist Power Convenings initiative at Yerba Buena Center for the Arts for the funding that allowed us to fund the classes and this anthology; to the amazing folks at the sites who have made the safe spaces for these elders to thrive: Lauren Bactad, Jessi Cutter, James Evans, Kate Kuckro, Marina Lazzara, Robert Sarison, and Geoffrey Washburn; to all of the teaching artists who facilitated the spaces for these writings to take place: Kevin Dublin, Antony Fangary, Meres-Sia Gabriel, Jessie Galloway, Michelle Kicherer, Tureeda Mikell, Christine No, Lucie Pereira, Tam Putnam, Denise Sullivan, Mary Gayle (MG) Thomas, and A.A. Vincent; to Dr. Adrienne Danyelle Oliver and Black Gold Storytellers for their partnership, to the co-directors of the program for their diligent copyediting and leadership: Kevin Dublin and Tam Putnam; to Jack Boulware, Jane Ganahl, Norah Piehl, Amy Kaminer, and Graham Todd for believing in and investing Litquake resources in the vision, to the readers near and far, listening to your elders; and most of all: to each of the senior writers, past, present, and future: ***thank you for sharing your stories***.

–The Co-Directors
Fall 2023

presented in partnership by

LITQUAKE

funded in part by

The
JOSEPH & VERA
LONG
Foundation

www.ingramcontent.com/pod-product-compliance
Lightning Source LLC
Chambersburg PA
CBHW061432210726
48287CB00007B/2174

* 9 7 8 1 9 3 5 8 4 7 1 9 9 *